STEEL'S

The Denver store at night, the Fontius Building (*Steel Sparks*, January 13, 1923)

STEEL'S

~ A ~

FORGOTTEN
STOCK MARKET
SCANDAL
FROM THE
1920s

Dave Dyer

Syracuse University Press

Syracuse, New York 13244-5290

First Edition 2013

13 14 15 16 17 18 6 5 4 3 2 1

∞ The paper used in this publication meets the minimum requirements of the American National Standard for Information Sciences—Permanence of Paper for Printed Library Materials, ANSI Z39.48-1992.

For a listing of books published and distributed by Syracuse University Press, visit our website at SyracuseUniversityPress.syr.edu.

ISBN: 978-0-8156-1012-0

Library of Congress Cataloging-in-Publication Data

Dyer, Dave.

Steel's : a forgotten stock market scandal from the 1920s /

Dave Dyer. — First edition.

pages cm

Includes bibliographical references and index.

ISBN 978-0-8156-1012-0 (cloth : alk. paper) 1. Steel, L. R, 1878–1923.
2. Investment advisors—United States—Case studies. 3. Fraud—United States—Case studies. 4. Ponzi schemes—United States—Case studies.
5. Financial services industry—Corrupt practices—United States—Case studies. I. Title.

HG4928.5.D94 2013

364.16'3092—dc23 2012050446

Manufactured in the United States of America

This book is dedicated to Clayton Evans Pickard, my great-uncle. He vanished in 1923 after working for Steel's, but he left just enough footprints for me to discover this amazing story.

Dave Dyer is an independent investor who lives in Houston, Texas. He has a master's degree in philosophy from the University of Michigan and spent twenty years in the software industry prior to investing and writing on a full-time basis. His publications include weekly stock market newsletters, newspaper editorials, and history articles for several magazines. He has been a frequent stock market commentator and radio talk show host for a business-oriented radio network. His e-mail address is davedyer@mindspring.com.

Contents

Illustrations

Preface

THEY SAY THAT HISTORY is written by the winners, but maybe it should not always be *about* the winners. The losers, especially the ones who had what it takes to win, can be fascinating. That idea certainly applies to the L. R. Steel Company, founded in Buffalo in 1919 and bankrupt by 1923, leaving sixty thousand investors about twenty-six million dollars poorer. This early chain store competitor of Woolworth's could have been Wal-Mart, but ended up being more like Enron.

This book came into existence because I discovered a long-lost treasure trove of internal company documents and photos from the L. R. Steel Company. It was a pure accident. I stumbled onto the documents while researching my great-uncle, Clayton Pickard, who vanished in 1923 after working for Steel's. I was interested only in finding out what happened to Clayton, but I found one of the biggest stock scandals in American history.

There were thousands of pages of company newsletters containing several thousand photos. It was like opening a time capsule that had been sealed since 1923. I was the first person to read them since they were bound and stored. I started reading them in a random fashion, as you might thumb through a magazine. I was drawn in by the creativity, enthusiasm, and foresight of this business. There were personal stories about employees, photos of customers and their children, accounts of elaborate parties and enthusiastic business meetings, and photos of bands playing at new store openings.

These documents were not just typical company newsletters. There were things that seemed odd for the times: women in management, a black man in a newspaper advertisement, and some employees over eighty years old. And a lot of big ideas: Could Niagara Falls really become the international center of commerce under Steel's direction? And why was a chain of retail stores producing a silent film about their business?

Throughout it all was the dynamic personality of Leonard Rambler Steel, the creative genius who founded the company.

I was hooked. I realized that I was being given an insider's view into an exceptionally creative and apparently successful company that was somehow involved in the disappearance of my great-uncle. I felt like I had opened a time capsule from the start of the Roaring Twenties that gave me a ringside seat into that exciting time.

I went back to the beginning and read them all in order. I just could not stop. Eventually, I digitized all the newsletters so that I could search the text. I found eleven references to Clayton Pickard.

The newsletters ended abruptly on February 17, 1923, but the story was not over. I read old newspapers, court records, and legal documents to see how it ended. I had no idea that I was reading about one of the biggest stock market scandals up to that time. My subsequent research revealed that more people lost money in Steel's that in Ponzi's scandal, although that fact seems to have been forgotten by history.

The remainder of this preface documents how my search for a lost ancestor uncovered these documents. Readers interested only in the results, and not my process, may prefer to skip to the first chapter.

Finding Clayton

"I wonder whatever happened to Clayton?" I grew up hearing my grandmother ask that question. Clayton Pickard, her only brother, had vanished without a trace sometime in the early 1920s and was never seen again. My grandmother lived to be ninety-three and never got an answer to her favorite question.

As I heard the story in the late 1950s when I was a kid, Clayton was due to show up for dinner at a cousin's home in Detroit and just never came. It was not normal behavior for him. He was a very responsible person and the one who really held the family together. He was close to his sister and her two young daughters. My mother, now ninety-seven, still talks about the big baskets of gifts that he would bring on Christmas and the giant chocolate bunnies that appeared at Easter. Plus, he was successful, over thirty, and married with three children. He was always viewed as the smartest person in the family and the one marked for success.

I also heard from both my mother and my grandmother that I was a lot like Clayton, by which they meant a good student and a poor athlete. And they kept saying that I even looked like him.

I grew up fascinated by Clayton. Did I really look like him? Did I inherit some of his nature? I certainly thought it possible that my great-uncle, Clayton, might somehow be my genetic twin. Would I someday vanish and leave an aura of mystery?

I asked a lot of questions, as most kids would. I was told there was a police report and that one of the wealthy cousins in Detroit hired a private detective. I was told that Clayton's French Canadian wife was contacted but was of no help. They had no idea where she and her children were now. My grandmother had lived in about twenty different cities over the previous thirty-five years as her husband's career as a construction superintendent took him from project to project, so it was understandable that contact had not been reestablished.

I speculated that someone had robbed him and threw him in the river, but my grandmother always felt that he was alive. She thought that perhaps something had gone wrong and he vanished on purpose. Clayton was always good with money; maybe he had been too good and disappeared with some embezzled funds. Then there was the story that he owned a big hotel in Florida. On the other hand, perhaps he had been excited by the 1917 revolution in Russia, abandoned his family, and moved to Russia to become a communist. There were persistent rumors of a scandal, but not too many details. In most of these fantasies, he was alive and wealthy, but there was never an explanation for why he never contacted his sister again. Sure, she lived in various cities over the years, but her husband worked for the same company, Stone & Webster, for forty years and Clayton could have easily found them. The Pickard family had lived in the same part of southern Ontario since the 1820s, and Clayton certainly would have been able to contact any number of cousins if he wanted to. Clayton even missed his mother's funeral in 1925.

However, a lot of families have family mysteries, and it is not unusual for them to go unsolved. Our mystery rested comfortably somewhere in the back of my mind for almost fifty years. Then, one day I had some spare time and decided to organize the old family photos. My grandmother had left me a few of Clayton, including one with his wife and children. My wife immediately commented that Clayton looked a lot like me, and I had to agree. Maybe my grandmother had been right about some other things as well.

With no grand plan, I set out to find Clayton. Genealogy is the new "killer application" on the Internet. Everyone has ancestors, and centuries full of their tracks have been digitized so that they are easily accessible. Research that previously would have required months of time looking through old newspapers or other documents can now be done in moments, frequently at no charge.

My initial search was simply to Google my grandmother's hometown, "Ingersoll, Ontario." I just wanted to see some pictures of it, but I was soon linked to an excellent site provided by Oxford County's local library, http://www.ocl.net/. The local history section had indexed all the birth, death, and marriage records from the local newspapers, and I soon found myself reading a detailed description of my grandmother's wedding in October 1910. Clayton was listed as one of the wedding party.

3. Clayton Pickard and his family in 1920

That quick initial success was not easily duplicated. There were a lot of blind alleys, false starts, and unworkable ideas. He was not listed in any Canadian or American census records, except as a child. The large Ancestry.com database did not include him. I found someone with the same name currently living in Tennessee; I sent him a letter on the off chance that he might be a son, but got no response.

My mother told me she thought that Clayton's son, probably named Peter, had become a priest in Quebec. I hired a researcher to go through some old records from the Catholic Church, but nothing turned up. I could not even find a researcher who would agree to help me find a Detroit police report from the 1920s. All agreed that it would be hopeless.

I made three assumptions based on stories from my mother and grandmother: he lived in Florida, he kept his name, and he started another family, so there were probably children or grandchildren who were related to him and could provide some details. All three of these assumptions turned out to be false.

While on vacation in Florida, I tried to track down the hotel rumor by searching city directories from the 1920s and 1930s. I thought I had found a needle in a haystack when I found someone managing a large Tampa hotel that had the last name of Pickard. However, I found that person's obituary, and the birth dates and details were so far off that I decided it was just a coincidence.

I finally got lucky while on another vacation, this time to our ancestral hometown of St. Marys, Ontario. It is a beautiful area, and the farm started in 1841 by my great-great-grandfather James Algernon Pickard is still in operation. My mother used to play there with Clayton's children. Ingersoll, where my grandmother grew up, is just a few miles away.

I went to Ingersoll to visit with the nice librarians at the Oxford County Library. They had been very generous with the time they took responding to my various requests, and they also had a very advanced computer operation for a small county library.

A casual remark by me advanced my search for Clayton. I said, "So what's new?" The helpful librarian said they had just added search capability to their online genealogy guest book so that it would be easy for people to connect with others researching the same family. I had signed the guest book and noted that I wanted information on Clayton Pickard, but nobody had ever contacted me. Standing at her desk, we searched the entire guest-book file for *Pickard* and found that Richard Pickard had visited while researching the Pickard family. I knew he must be related to me, and he was. His e-mail address was in the address book, so I contacted him.

He turned out to be Clayton's grandson and my second cousin. About the same age, Richard and I probably would have known each other growing up if Clayton had been around to keep the family closer. Richard's father was the small boy in the earlier family photo, the one my mom thought was a priest. So much for my mom's rumors.

I found out that Richard's father (named Ed, not Peter as my mom thought) was in his eighties and doing well. Unfortunately, Ed had not seen his father since he was five years old, and Clayton Pickard was as much of a mystery to his family as he was to me.

I visited them in Ottawa and picked up some valuable leads. Ed said that Clayton and his family lived in Buffalo; that city was the last place he ever saw them. I had wasted a lot of time looking in Florida, so this gave me a chance to start over in a new place. In fact, Ed, as an adult, had visited Buffalo in an attempt to locate his lost father.

I got another important lead from this trip: Clayton had worked for the L. R. Steel Company. They even had a copy of a company newsletter that had an article about him.

It was a detailed biography of Clayton as a young chain store executive. His career and abilities were described in glowing terms. One minor detail caught my attention: since one of his responsibilities was to act as the candy buyer for all the stores, I knew where those big chocolate Easter bunnies that my mother recalls came from. It was one of those "aha moments" that can come from finding a connection between unrelated facts that really mean nothing to other people. I filed the article away with the thought that I might look into the history of this company, if possible, and get some insight about his later life.

I refocused my search on finding Clayton in Buffalo. After a few more dead ends, I decided to see if perhaps someone had misspelled his name. Sometimes, the *k* is left out, and *Pickard* becomes *Picard.* It was the lucky guess that unlocked many doors.

IN CHARGE OF STEEL STORES IN UNITED STATES

Clayton E. Pickard

The destinies of the L. R. Steel Company 5 cents to $1 stores in the United States are in the hands of a man whose ability and past experience leave no question as to the success of these thrift marts. That man is Clayton E. Pickard, recognized as one of the best of chain store executives.

From early youth, Mr. Pickard has been identified with the chain store industry. His entry into the business world was at the age of 16, when he entered the employ of the Traders Bank at Leamington, Ont. After three years of bank experience, during which he held various positions, he turned to the field of chain store merchandising, and accepted employment in the stock room of S. H. Knox & Co., in London, Ont. Since that time Mr. Pickard had experienced many changes in positions in the business of the Knox and F. W. Woolworth stores, and each change had marked a step upward in station and responsibility. His ability was soon recognized by those in authority, and as a consequence his promotion was rapid and steady.

On November 1, 1919, Mr. Pickard became associated with the L. R. Steel Company, Ltd., assuming the position of buyer for the Canadian stores, with offices in Toronto. He remained in that capacity until February of this year, when he was appointed general manager of the L. R. Steel 5 cents to $1 stores in the United States, transferring his headquarters to the executive offices in Buffalo.

In addition to the general direction of the stores in the United States, Mr. Pickard acts in the capacity of buyer for candy, notions, jewelry, stationery and other goods handled in the stores.

During his service with the Knox and Woolworth stores, Mr. Pickard originated many selling ideas, and many of his innovations, after introducing them in the stores where he was serving, were quickly adopted and used throughout the chain of stores.

4. *Steel Sparks*, September 18, 1920

I got a hit immediately on his Social Security death record. I sent off to get a copy of his original application, and the birth date matched, so it was clearly him. The difference was that, by 1939, when he filled out the Social Security forms, he decided to change his last name to Picard. He even had a new signature. It is interesting to contrast this signature with the more florid and elegant signature from 1910 when, at twenty, he was a witness to his sister's wedding.

He had obviously changed the spelling of his name on purpose. My guess about a misspelling had been wrong, but lucky. In retrospect, if you were going to change your name, it would be best to change only one letter so that you would not need to learn a new signature. In those precomputer days, your distinctive signature was like your password.

Now that I had the new name for Clayton, I was able to find his obituary. He died in 1962 at age seventy-two, and, oddly, a

5. Clayton's signature on his 1939 Social Security application

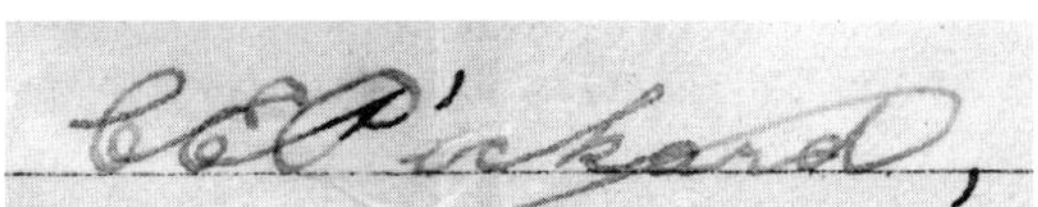

6. Clayton's signature in 1910

woman named Helen was listed as his sister, although other information was accurate. Clearly false, but interesting.

A final bit of luck shed some light on this new mystery. Without going into all the details, I used the Ancestry.com surname message boards (luckily, Helen did not have a common last name) to get in contact with Helen's granddaughter who actually knew Clayton.

He was the "mystery man" who lived with her grandmother, but was really part of the family. Helen was a widow with three kids, and Clayton moved in as her unofficial boyfriend. He was involved in their lives, and perhaps this new family took the place of the real family that he never saw again.

The granddaughter said that Clayton presented himself as being French Canadian and spoke fluent French. He supported himself as a contractor who did the interiors of movie theaters, and he was occasionally

7. Clayton later in his life

in partnership with a local mural painter. He never talked about his prior life, and she was surprised to find out about it. They were able to provide me with a photo of Clayton as a mature adult. I visited Buffalo to see where he lived, to do some more in-person research, and to just get a feeling for his life.

There was just one more step in the process. I needed to tell Clayton's son about the life of the father that he had not seen since he was five. That was the best part of my search.

I found out more about Clayton than I had ever hoped, but I still did not know why he changed his name and never attempted to see his family again. Clearly, something in his life had gone very wrong.

Then I recalled the company he worked for, the L. R. Steel Company, which had published the newsletter with the article about his career. Perhaps I could find out something about them that would shed some light on Clayton's behavior.

8. The author in Quebec with Clayton's son, Ed

Finding the Newsletters

I went to Buffalo to visit Clayton's grave and see his old home. Since I had some spare time one evening in the hotel, I decided to Google the L. R. Steel Company as a starting point. I do not recall the exact search term, but I got many pages of irrelevant responses. Some were about steel rims for Land Rovers; others were about companies engaged in the steel business. Then there was L. R. Steel Cut Oatmeal. With time on my hands, I scrolled through them all. Six or seven pages deep, I saw an eBay listing that was described as "Americana." An antique dealer from Rochester, New York, was selling a box of newsletters from the L. R. Steel Company. The auction was still open with no bids, but it had a "Buy It Now" option. I bought them immediately for about fifty dollars plus shipping, hoping to find some more references to Clayton.

When the twenty-pound box arrived at my front door, I was not prepared for the time capsule of details about a rapidly growing company that was led by an energetic young visionary named Leonard Rambler Steel. The internal view of the rise and fall of this early competitor in the chain store market included thousands of photographs of people and places that had not seen the light of day in more than eighty-five years.

There were detailed stories about individual employees and customers. There were group photographs of meetings, banquets, store openings, and company outings. There were articles on company strategy and sales promotions.

The photographs were stunning and documented with extensive detail about the subjects. I realized immediately what a hidden treasure these newsletters were for anyone with ancestors who were involved with the company. Because the L. R. Steel Company had sixty thousand investors, at least five thousand employees, and thousands of customers, there ought to be many people who would love to access these newsletters.

I contacted the antique dealer to see if he had any information about the provenance of the newsletters, but he could not recall where he got them. However, he thought he had a second box, and I arranged to buy it as soon as he found it. I soon had my second twenty-pound box.

The name S. F. Head was on the outside of the binder that held the newsletters. The editor was Samuel F. Head, so I must have the editor's personal stash. That fact would explain why they are in such wonderful condition with no signs of wear or use. An article about Samuel F. Head also explained why the newsletters had such a professional appearance: he had been the city editor for one of the local newspapers for six years prior to joining Steel's.

In all, I have 136 newsletters, and each one is about twenty pages long, so there are almost three thousand pages. To make them more usable, I scanned each one and created a set of .pdf files that contain about 525 megabytes of data that are all searchable with the text search tool included

SAMUEL F. HEAD JOINS THE HOUSE OF STEEL

Samuel F. Head, for the past six years city editor of The Buffalo Enquirer, and who has been devoting part time for the past two months in assisting Mr. Rudulph on "Steel Sparks," has re-signed his position on The Enquirer to become assistant to Mr. Rudulph in the publicity department of the L. R. Steel Service Corporation of New York and the L. R. Steel Companies in the United States and Canada.

Mr. Head's long experience as a newspaper man has equipped him for the work he will undertake and, as he was associated with Mr. Rudulph when the latter was managing editor of The Enquirer, he is familiar with his methods and desires. He played an important part in connection with the extra edition issued by The Enquirer and circulated at the banquet held during the convention. He joins the House of Steel upon Mr. Rudulph's recommendation, and the latter is confident he will prove to be a valuable addition to the publicity department.

9. *Steel Sparks,* October 16, 1920

in the Adobe Acrobat Reader. The earliest one was published on May 29, 1920. It is listed as volume 1, number 5, so I may have missed the first four issues. The last one I have was published on February 17, 1923.

The newsletters were directed to the sales force, which at one point comprised around five thousand people all over the United States and Canada, but it was also provided to customers. Since the customers were considered owners of the company, this openness is understandable, but most companies today would prefer to keep their sales documents internal.

Like everything else that L. R. Steel did, the newsletters were produced as if money was not a concern. He hired a full-time artist to make sure that the weekly newsletters looked professional. The artist also produced a large number of cartoons that add a certain flair to the publication.

Throughout all the newsletters, there is a sense of optimism and energy that was entirely appropriate for the start of the Roaring Twenties.

OUR ARTIST AND A SAMPLE OF HIS WORK

Clyde W. DuVall, staff artist, about whom more will be heard later, has been confining himself to work on forthcoming prospectness but will shortly be able to devote considerable time to "STEEL SPARKS." Mr. DuVall is a life-long resident of Buffalo and has been engaged in art work for the past six years. As pictorial designer for the DuVall Art company, his work attracted wide attention. When the war was in progress he had the honor of being the youngest officer in the United States navy. He was in the service over two years. For eight months he had charge of the drafting department at Harvard University and was later transferred to the Great Lakes Training station at Chicago. Upon his return to Buffalo he became identified with the Buffalo Electrotype company and has been an instructor in the city's vocational schools. He assumed charge of the art department of the L. R. STEEL SERVICE CORPORATION about a month ago.

CLYDE DUVALL

10. The art department (*Steel Sparks,* May 29, 1920)

11. The *Steel Sparks* logo: Honesty, Loyalty, and Truth

The creative energy of the founder is evident on every page. L. R. Steel was clearly more interesting than my great-uncle, Clayton. This virtual time capsule that I found by accident told the fascinating story about a forgotten company that impacted many lives, not just Clayton's.

Acknowledgments

I WISH TO THANK the following people and organizations who assisted my research:

Wilma and Roy McQuown and Mildred Bell. They are descendants of the Steel family who greatly assisted with the research.

Buffalo and Erie County Historical Society. I spent time researching their records for anything relating to Steel's.

Buffalo and Erie County Public Library. The Grosvenor Room has a large and well-organized collection of newspapers, scrapbooks, and city directories that I used extensively. The local history card catalog had several items about L. R. Steel.

Western New York Heritage Press and Douglas W. DeCroix, executive editor. A subset of my research was published in the fall 2009 issue of their magazine under the title "The Man Who Did Almost Everything Right."

The National Archives in New York City and Kansas. They provided me with an opportunity to review the original bankruptcy records.

Ancestry.com. They are an indispensable database of genealogical data and also an excellent way to contact other researchers. I could never have found Clayton's second family without using their message boards.

Google Books. They helped me find a legal reference from the 1920s that had been digitized.

New York Times Archive. I purchased twenty-six contemporary newspaper articles about Steel's from this site.

My wife, Lorraine Cherry, PhD. She edited early versions of this book.

Don Morris, PhD, of the University of Illinois at Springfield. He provided the insight that failure is particularly interesting to study when the person who failed had what it takes to succeed.

Professor Ed Blair, chairman of the Department of Marketing and Entrepreneurship at the University of Houston for assistance in researching some marketing concepts discussed in the book.

My Canadian cousins Richard Pickard and Marilyn Sandiford and their father, Ed Pickard. They provided valuable insights and excellent motivation.

Pat Graesser, another Canadian cousin. Her expertise in genealogy helped with my research.

Toledo-Lucas County Public Library. They provided the contemporary newspaper accounts of L. R.'s death.

Boston Globe. They provided contemporary newspaper accounts of the Ponzi scheme.

Oxford County Public Library, Ingersoll, Ontario. A wonderful library that got me started with my research.

Clayton Library Center for Genealogical Research, part of the Houston Public Library system. They provided interlibrary loan services for items that I ordered from other libraries.

Claudia Dyer, my mom, who put up with my many questions about Clayton.

Erie County Surrogate's Court. They helped me search for Clayton's will, but none was filed.

US District Court in Buffalo. The court assisted in the search for immigration records; none were found.

Erie County Clerk's Office. They responded to my numerous requests, both in person and on the phone, for legal documents relating to Steel's.

William Henderson. He provided information about the subsequent owner of Marguerite Manor.

Ken Schroeppel, urban planner with Matrix Design Group who helped me understand the current status of Steel's building in Denver.

Mount Calvary Cemetery, Cheektowaga, New York, and Forest Lawn Cemetery, Buffalo. They helped in locating the graves of Clayton Pickard and Leonard Rambler Steel.

Dr. Harold Griffin. He advised me on a medical condition exhibited by one of Steel's employees.

Shane Burris of the Pennsylvania State University Interlibrary Loan Department. He helped by digitizing an out-of-copyright book that I requested.

STEEL'S

1

The Man Who Did Almost Everything Right

The Right Business at the Right Time in the Right Place

IN THE EARLY 1920S, Buffalo residents saw plenty of well-dressed "Steelites" driving new cars and eating at the best restaurants. Their offices had fresh flowers every day. And they all had a certain peppy attitude, possibly from the motivational meeting that started each day at the office. They beamed with the confidence of people convinced that they were helping humanity and making a lot of money in the process. And they loved Leonard Rambler Steel, the man who made it all possible.

Leonard Rambler Steel did almost everything right. Almost. He started the right business at the right time in the right place, and he was the right guy to do it.

Chain stores were the hot new business concept in the early twentieth century. They changed retailing just as much as Amazon.com and eBay did in the late 1990s. Chain stores provided opportunities for the energetic young entrepreneurs, and the successful ones, like Frank W. Woolworth, were among the wealthiest people in the world. When Woolworth's sixty-story building was dedicated in Manhattan on April 24, 1913, it was the tallest building in existence and a proclamation that chain stores could produce extreme wealth. Bright, optimistic young people like L. R. Steel (as he liked to be called) flowed into this business just as they did into the Internet start-ups.

Chain stores were successful because they were able to provide a wide variety of merchandise to customers at lower prices than competitors. Because they bought for multiple stores in large lots directly from the factory, they could eliminate the expense of a wholesaler that must be used for lower-volume purchasers. The lower selling prices led to faster inventory turnover than in independently owned stores, so the small,

12. Leonard Rambler Steel (*Steel Sparks,* November 5, 1921)

older stores were outcompeted on both price and selection. Also, centralized administration of multiple stores had the advantage of consistency and adaptability. Lessons learned in one store could be implemented elsewhere quickly.

In addition to economies of scale, chain stores fostered new merchandizing techniques. Prior to chain stores, merchandise was hidden behind a counter or out of sight in drawers. Not only was it a labor-intensive operation for an employee to show merchandise to a customer, but this arrangement intimidated some shoppers and discouraged impulse buying. Chain stores brought the goods out in the open where they could be inspected by shoppers without the assistance of a clerk. This change not only cut down on the need for clerks, but improved the shopping experience for the customers.

The August 5, 1922, issue of the company newsletter, *Steel Sparks,* reprinted an article from the *Montreal Financial Times* extolling the chain store concept in general and referring to Steel's success in particular.

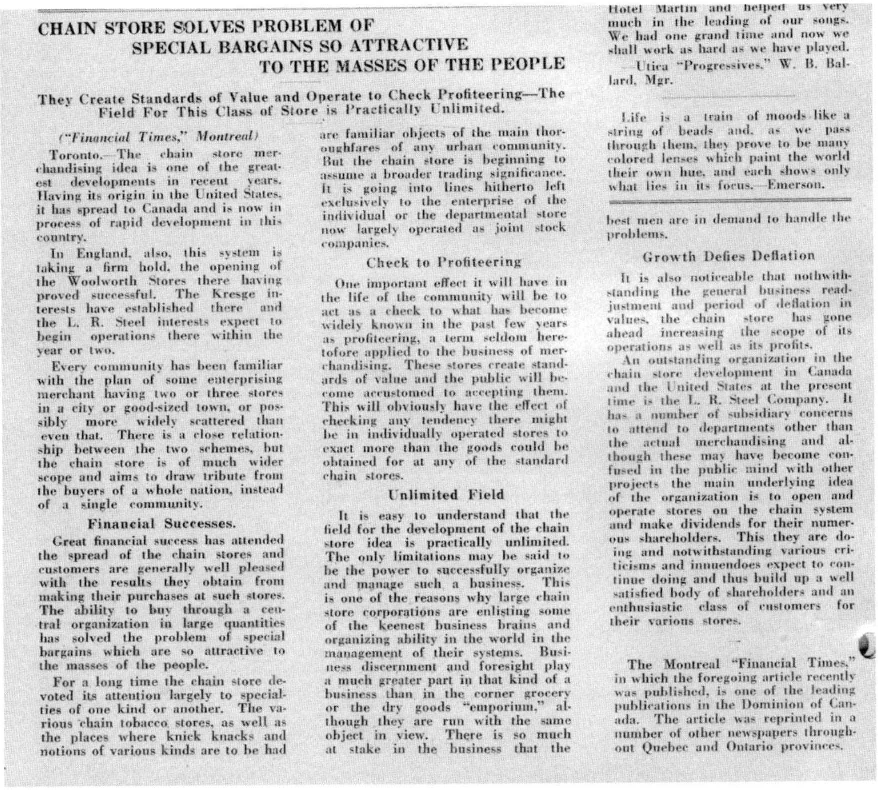

Hotel Martin and helped us very much in the leading of our songs. We had one grand time and now we shall work as hard as we have played.

—Utica "Progressives," W. B. Ballard, Mgr.

Life is a train of moods like a string of beads and, as we pass through them, they prove to be many colored lenses which paint the world their own hue, and each shows only what lies in its focus.—Emerson.

CHAIN STORE SOLVES PROBLEM OF SPECIAL BARGAINS SO ATTRACTIVE TO THE MASSES OF THE PEOPLE

They Create Standards of Value and Operate to Check Profiteering—The Field For This Class of Store is Practically Unlimited.

("*Financial Times,*" *Montreal*)

Toronto.—The chain store merchandising idea is one of the greatest developments in recent years. Having its origin in the United States, it has spread to Canada and is now in process of rapid development in this country.

In England, also, this system is taking a firm hold, the opening of the Woolworth Stores there having proved successful. The Kresge interests have established there and the L. R. Steel interests expect to begin operations there within the year or two.

Every community has been familiar with the plan of some enterprising merchant having two or three stores in a city or good-sized town, or possibly more widely scattered than even that. There is a close relationship between the two schemes, but the chain store is of much wider scope and aims to draw tribute from the buyers of a whole nation, instead of a single community.

Financial Successes.

Great financial success has attended the spread of the chain stores and customers are generally well pleased with the results they obtain from making their purchases at such stores. The ability to buy through a central organization in large quantities has solved the problem of special bargains which are so attractive to the masses of the people.

For a long time the chain store devoted its attention largely to specialties of one kind or another. The various chain tobacco stores, as well as the places where knick knacks and notions of various kinds are to be had are familiar objects of the main thoroughfares of any urban community. But the chain store is beginning to assume a broader trading significance. It is going into lines hitherto left exclusively to the enterprise of the individual or the departmental store now largely operated as joint stock companies.

Check to Profiteering

One important effect it will have in the life of the community will be to act as a check to what has become widely known in the past few years as profiteering, a term seldom heretofore applied to the business of merchandising. These stores create standards of value and the public will become accustomed to accepting them. This will obviously have the effect of checking any tendency there might be in individually operated stores to exact more than the goods could be obtained for at any of the standard chain stores.

Unlimited Field

It is easy to understand that the field for the development of the chain store idea is practically unlimited. The only limitations may be said to be the power to successfully organize and manage such a business. This is one of the reasons why large chain store corporations are enlisting some of the keenest business brains and organizing ability in the world in the management of their systems. Business discernment and foresight play a much greater part in that kind of a business than in the corner grocery or the dry goods "emporium," although they are run with the same object in view. There is so much at stake in the business that the best men are in demand to handle the problems.

Growth Defies Deflation

It is also noticeable that nothwithstanding the general business readjustment and period of deflation in values, the chain store has gone ahead increasing the scope of its operations as well as its profits.

An outstanding organization in the chain store development in Canada and the United States at the present time is the L. R. Steel Company. It has a number of subsidiary concerns to attend to departments other than the actual merchandising and although these may have become confused in the public mind with other projects the main underlying idea of the organization is to open and operate stores on the chain system and make dividends for their numerous shareholders. This they are doing and notwithstanding various criticisms and innuendoes expect to continue doing and thus build up a well satisfied body of shareholders and an enthusiastic class of customers for their various stores.

The Montreal "Financial Times," in which the foregoing article recently was published, is one of the leading publications in the Dominion of Canada. The article was reprinted in a number of other newspapers throughout Quebec and Ontario provinces.

13. The advantages of chain stores (*Steel Sparks,* August 5, 1922)

L. R. founded his company on October 19, 1919, just as the Roaring Twenties were about to begin. The timing was perfect. It was a magical time when anything seemed possible. The Great War had ended one year earlier, and consumers were ready to forget the frugality of the war years. There had been an economic slump immediately after the war ended in November 1918, because factories that had been running overtime on war contracts started reductions as those contracts were canceled (Allen 1931, 7). However, these workers soon moved on to find employment in new industries, such as retail chain stores. Many of the employees at Steel's were returning military people. When they needed a photo for an article about them in *Steel Sparks,* many of them provided their recent military photos.

As Warren G. Harding said in the presidential campaign of 1920, America needed a return to "normalcy." L. R. echoed this effective political campaign slogan in a message celebrating Harding's inauguration: "The House of Steel will reap the benefits it deserves in the onward march back to normal times. Having accomplished what marked its rapid progress when clouds obscured the sun, who can predict what its share will be with the sun shining in all its glory?" (*Steel Sparks*, March 5, 1921).

ANOTHER DECORATION FOR HERBERT BESWICK

Herbert Beswick, a fine, fearless, young man of London, Ontario, has been decorated with the Steel Service button for selling 24 shares during his first week with the London office.

Young Mr. Beswick has a wonderful war record. He was one of the heroes on the valiant ship "Vindictive" that made the famous naval raid on the enemy's submarine base at Zeebrugge during the world war.

He was personally congratulated by Sir Arthur Currie, commander of the Canadian forces.

He is a valuable acquisition to Manager Broadbendt's London staff. Herbert Beswick has the courage and backbone to stick, strive, smile and conquer the hardest tasks.

14. War hero to salesman (*Steel Sparks*, November 6, 1920)

"Normalcy" meant commerce, innovation, and prosperity to Americans. Three of the innovations that created whole new industries in the postwar decade were radio, movies, and the automobile. All three of these developments helped to create an economic environment that was driven by consumer demand. The marketplace was very receptive of the new retail innovations brought by chain stores.

The first commercial radio station, KDKA in Pittsburgh, opened just in time to broadcast Harding's victory on November 2, 1920 (Allen 1931, 67). Within a couple of years, radio seized the public's imagination.

Automobiles, even if the roads were not ready for them, and movies, even without sound, created business opportunities. As we shall see, L. R. found a very creative way to use movies to promote his business.

In addition to being in the right business at the right time, L. R. was in the right place. Buffalo was a boomtown when he started his business. The population of Buffalo in 1920 was 506,775 (US Census Bureau 1998), making it the eleventh largest city in America at that time (Infoplease 2011). By 2000 the population had declined to 292,648 (US Census Bureau 2000).

Buffalo's dynamic and growing economy benefited from a location that made it a great inland port at the eastern end of the Great Lakes. Iron ore from Minnesota, grain and cattle from the fertile Midwest, all were shipped by water through Buffalo on their way to the industrial centers of the East Coast. Buffalo became the largest grain port in the world and was second only to Chicago in livestock shipments (Allen 1931, 38).

Because the goods finished their trip to the East Coast by rail, Buffalo became a major railroad hub and was second only to Chicago in rail traffic (ibid., 40). If the St. Lawrence Seaway, which opened in 1959, had not provided a more convenient all-water route from the Midwest to the Atlantic coast, Buffalo might be as large as Chicago today.

The final element in Buffalo's early economic success was abundant, inexpensive electricity from Niagara Falls. Heavy industry grew rapidly in this business-friendly environment. The older industries (steel, grain, and lumber) provided economic stability and employed more people, but the new industries (airplanes, chemicals, and automobiles) provided dynamic growth. More than half of all the American airplanes used in World War I were made by two Buffalo companies, Curtiss and Wright (ibid., 84). Steel's company newsletter contained these observations about Buffalo's excellent location:

> Niagara Falls lies at the center of the most important industrial area of the North American Continent. It eclipses in this respect even the greatest metropolis of the world, New York, and the greatest city of the Mississippi Valley, Chicago.

> Niagara Falls is even today the greatest center for electric power and for the electro-chemical industries in the world. It has unusual facilities for rail and water transportation and these facilities will be steadily improved under pressure of the inexorable demands of commerce and industry.
>
> Electric power, based on water power, will be the mighty, cheap power of the future. Niagara lies at the heart of the greatest water power region of the world.
>
> Every facility for transportation, communication, and recreation which modern ingenuity has discovered will be provided for those who come to carry on business or to worship at the magnificent shrine which Nature has given mankind. (*Steel Sparks,* October 21, 1922)

Buffalo in the early 1920s attracted many young entrepreneurs like L. R., but he was one of the best. It helped to be in the right place at the right time, but he was also the right guy to be there. Success came naturally to him.

He had a beautiful home in Buffalo on Lafayette Avenue that is still lovely, but he spent most of his time at his palatial country home on Getzville Road, near Ellicott Creek on the northern edge of Buffalo. This home was named Marguerite Manor, after his wife. It had a tennis court, bowling alley, and swimming pool and was the site of many business gatherings.

L. R. was a creative visionary and a dreamer, but he was also a dynamic force with a lot of practical experience. His story is the familiar one of the small-town boy who did well through hard work, dedication, and singular focus.

He grew up in Middletown, Pennsylvania, a town of about five thousand at the time of his birth in 1878. The town is along the Susquehanna River in the southeast part of the state, only a few miles from the Three Mile Island Nuclear Power Plant. There must have been something in the air back then that promoted chain stores because the very first Woolworth's was founded in 1879 just thirty miles away, in Lancaster (Plunkett-Powell 1999, 45).

As a child, his favorite game was "playing store," and he shipped his goods over an imaginary railroad. At fourteen, he was working in a store.

15. L. R.'s city home in Buffalo

16. Marguerite Manor, the country home (*Steel Sparks*, July 15, 1922)

He swept it out in the morning before school and returned to make deliveries after school.

By the time he was twenty, in 1898, he owned a small stationery store in Middletown, where he got his first taste of boom times. The Spanish-American War had just begun, and Camp George Meade, on the outskirts

17. L. R.'s parents and family home (*Steel Sparks,* October 7, 1922)

of Middletown, filled with soldiers. When the troops arrived at the train station, they were greeted by the young L. R. offering them free sandwiches and fruit. His instincts were perfect. Seeing an opportunity, he changed his business to include fruit, candy, and sandwiches. Then he expanded to open a restaurant. His business was so brisk that he was able to order fruit by the boxcar at significant discounts.

He soon learned the risks of depending on a wartime boom. The camp, which had been opened in August, was closed in November when the troops were sent south for the winter. He saw the crisis coming and did what many entrepreneurs do when facing financial ruin: he looked for a job.

He was hired by Foster, Post & Company, a small chain store operator based in Saginaw, Michigan. At that time, they had four stores, all in Michigan. L. R. went to work in the Flint, Michigan, store.

He gained experience and moved up the ladder quickly while living in Duluth, Terre Haute, Bloomington, and Pittsburgh. By the time he was twenty-four, he was inspector of stores for the Siebert-Good Company in Chicago. There were rapid promotions based on his obvious management ability. As it is for a young dot-comer in Silicon Valley, it was easy to change jobs. He worked for many of the well-known chains of the day: Kresge, Woolworth's, and S. H. Knox. He stayed with Knox for a year, but left when he found that stock was reserved for the "insiders" and he was not one of them. At one point, he started his own chain of six stores, but ended up selling them to Woolworth's because he did not have sufficient capital to manage them.

He then had a longer career at Metropolitan Stores, a chain with eighty-nine locations. He rose to become the general manager but left in a huff when he was passed over for the presidency in favor of a Wall Street banker.

He was almost forty when he started his own chain for the second time. This time he had more capital, more experience, and, most important, his Big Idea that would be the basis for his empire: if the customers actually owned the stores, why would they ever shop anywhere else?

Selling stock directly to the public provided him with both investment capital and loyal customers. This idea proved to be a big winner, in fact more successful than the stores themselves. By June 1922, he had 225 business locations, including sales offices, five-and-dime stores, candy shops, and cafeterias. He had more than forty-five hundred employees and forty thousand investors.

His stock-selling organization was called the L. R. Steel Service Company, because the salesmen were providing a service to the customers by introducing them to this great investment. The service company had offices all over the United States and Canada. Of course, they sold stock on an installment plan to make it easier on everyone.

His ideas were good, but his leadership skills were spectacular. A story from the December 24, 1920, issue of *Steel Sparks* does an excellent job of illustrating L. R.'s combination of boyish enthusiasm and leadership ability. On Sunday, December 19, a group of managers from the eastern and central districts of the Realty Division were in Buffalo for an all-day meeting. An all-day meeting away from home on the Sunday before Christmas could not have been very popular. As the meeting droned on, Steel made an unannounced appearance:

18. The Big Idea (*Steel Sparks,* September 15, 1922)

Mr. Steel literally broke up the meeting temporarily. After acknowledging the greeting extended him, he invited all to accompany him across the street to inspect the new Steel Cafeteria at 297 Washington, which is in the last stages of preparation for its formal opening. Mr. Steel expressed in word and manner his justified pride in the remarkable institution. As the party moved through the cafeteria, marveling at the beauty, serviceability and completeness of the equipment, Mr. Steel halted occasionally to relate new and each time more wonderful accomplishments in the line of business deals and property acquisitions of benefit to the House of Steel. The enthusiasm of the members of the party mounted steadily as they made the tour of inspection and listened to Mr. Steel.

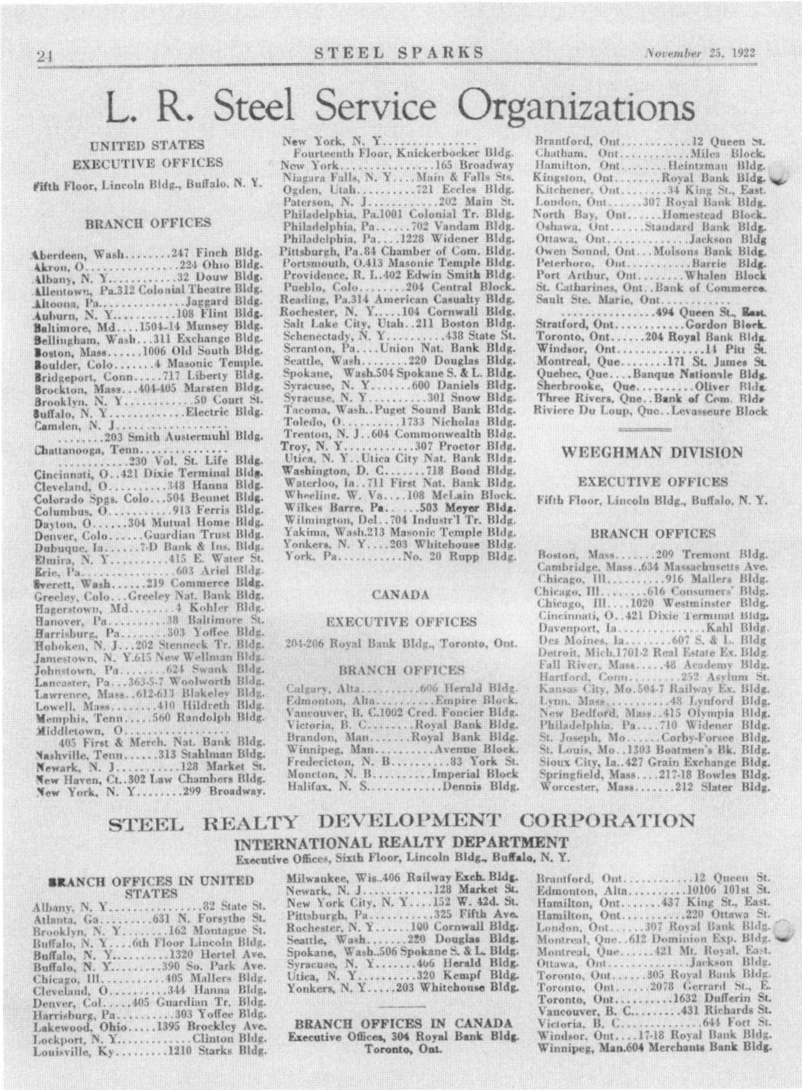

24 STEEL SPARKS *November 25, 1922*

L. R. Steel Service Organizations

UNITED STATES

EXECUTIVE OFFICES

Fifth Floor, Lincoln Bldg., Buffalo, N. Y.

BRANCH OFFICES

Aberdeen, Wash........247 Finch Bldg.
Akron, O...............224 Ohio Bldg.
Albany, N. Y............32 Douw Bldg.
Allentown, Pa.312 Colonial Theatre Bldg.
Altoona, Pa...............Jaggard Bldg.
Auburn, N. Y...........108 Flint Bldg.
Baltimore, Md....1504-14 Munsey Bldg.
Bellingham, Wash...311 Exchange Bldg.
Boston, Mass......1006 Old South Bldg.
Boulder, Colo.......4 Masonic Temple.
Bridgeport, Conn.....717 Liberty Bldg.
Brockton, Mass...404-405 Marsten Bldg.
Brooklyn, N. Y............50 Court St.
Buffalo, N. Y............Electric Bldg.
Camden, N. J..................
........203 Smith Austermuhl Bldg.
Chattanooga, Tenn..............
...........230 Vol. St. Life Bldg.
Cincinnati, O..421 Dixie Terminal Bldg.
Cleveland, O...........348 Hanna Bldg.
Colorado Spgs. Colo...504 Bennet Bldg.
Columbus, O...........913 Ferris Bldg.
Dayton, O......304 Mutual Home Bldg.
Denver, Colo......Guardian Trust Bldg.
Dubuque, Ia.......7-D Bank & Ins. Bldg.
Elmira, N. Y..........415 E. Water St.
Erie, Pa.................603 Ariel Bldg.
Everett, Wash......219 Commerce Bldg.
Greeley, Colo...Greeley Nat. Bank Bldg.
Hagerstown, Md........4 Kohler Bldg.
Hanover, Pa...........38 Baltimore St.
Harrisburg, Pa.........303 Yoffee Bldg.
Hoboken, N. J...202 Stenneck Tr. Bldg.
Jamestown, N. Y.615 New Wellman Bldg.
Johnstown, Pa........624 Swank Bldg.
Lancaster, Pa...363-5-7 Woolworth Bldg.
Lawrence, Mass..612-613 Blakeley Bldg.
Lowell, Mass.........410 Hildreth Bldg.
Memphis, Tenn.....560 Randolph Bldg.
Middletown, O..................
405 First & Merch. Nat. Bank Bldg.
Nashville, Tenn......313 Stahlman Bldg.
Newark, N. J...........128 Market St.
New Haven, Ct..302 Law Chambers Bldg.
New York, N. Y........299 Broadway.
New York, N. Y...............
Fourteenth Floor, Knickerbocker Bldg.
New York................165 Broadway
Niagara Falls, N. Y....Main & Falls Sts.
Ogden, Utah..........721 Eccles Bldg.
Paterson, N. J............202 Main St.
Philadelphia, Pa.1001 Colonial Tr. Bldg.
Philadelphia, Pa......702 Vandam Bldg.
Philadelphia, Pa....1228 Widener Bldg.
Pittsburgh, Pa.84 Chamber of Com. Bldg.
Portsmouth, O.413 Masonic Temple Bldg.
Providence, R. I..402 Edwin Smith Bldg.
Pueblo, Colo........204 Central Block.
Reading, Pa.314 American Casualty Bldg.
Rochester, N. Y.....104 Cornwall Bldg.
Salt Lake City, Utah..211 Boston Bldg.
Schenectady, N. Y..........438 State St.
Scranton, Pa....Union Nat. Bank Bldg.
Seattle, Wash........220 Douglas Bldg.
Spokane, Wash.504 Spokane S. & L. Bldg.
Syracuse, N. Y.......600 Daniels Bldg.
Syracuse, N. Y..........301 Snow Bldg.
Tacoma, Wash..Puget Sound Bank Bldg.
Toledo, O..........1733 Nicholas Bldg.
Trenton, N. J..604 Commonwealth Bldg.
Troy, N. Y............307 Proctor Bldg.
Utica, N. Y..Utica City Nat. Bank Bldg.
Washington, D. C.......718 Bond Bldg.
Waterloo, Ia..711 First Nat. Bank Bldg.
Wheeling, W. Va....108 McLain Block.
Wilkes Barre, Pa......503 Meyer Bldg.
Wilmington, Del..704 Industr'l Tr. Bldg.
Yakima, Wash.213 Masonic Temple Bldg.
Yonkers, N. Y....203 Whitehouse Bldg.
York, Pa...........No. 20 Rupp Bldg.

CANADA

EXECUTIVE OFFICES

204-206 Royal Bank Bldg., Toronto, Ont.

BRANCH OFFICES

Calgary, Alta..........606 Herald Bldg.
Edmonton, Alta..........Empire Block.
Vancouver, B. C.1002 Cred. Foncier Bldg.
Victoria, B. C........Royal Bank Bldg.
Brandon, Man.......Royal Bank Bldg.
Winnipeg, Man..........Avenue Block.
Fredericton, N. B..........83 York St.
Moncton, N. B..........Imperial Block
Halifax, N. S............Dennis Bldg.
Brantford, Ont............12 Queen St.
Chatham, Ont............Miles Block.
Hamilton, Ont........Heintzman Bldg.
Kingston, Ont........Royal Bank Bldg.
Kitchener, Ont........34 King St., East.
London, Ont......307 Royal Bank Bldg.
North Bay, Ont......Homestead Block.
Oshawa, Ont......Standard Bank Bldg.
Ottawa, Ont..............Jackson Bldg
Owen Sound, Ont...Molsons Bank Bldg.
Peterboro, Ont...........Barrie Bldg.
Port Arthur, Ont........Whalen Block
St. Catharines, Ont..Bank of Commerce.
Sault Ste. Marie, Ont...........
..................494 Queen St., East.
Stratford, Ont.............Gordon Block.
Toronto, Ont......204 Royal Bank Bldg.
Windsor, Ont...............14 Pitt St.
Montreal, Que........171 St. James St.
Quebec, Que....Banque Nationale Bldg.
Sherbrooke, Que..........Oliver Bldg.
Three Rivers, Que..Bank of Com. Bldg.
Riviere Du Loup, Que..Levasseure Block

WEEGHMAN DIVISION

EXECUTIVE OFFICES

Fifth Floor, Lincoln Bldg., Buffalo, N. Y.

BRANCH OFFICES

Boston, Mass.......209 Tremont Bldg.
Cambridge, Mass..634 Massachusetts Ave.
Chicago, Ill..........916 Mallers Bldg.
Chicago, Ill........616 Consumers' Bldg.
Chicago, Ill....1020 Westminster Bldg.
Cincinnati, O..421 Dixie Terminal Bldg.
Davenport, Ia...................Kahl Bldg.
Des Moines, Ia........607 S. & L. Bldg
Detroit, Mich.1701-2 Real Estate Ex. Bldg.
Fall River, Mass.....48 Academy Bldg.
Hartford, Conn.........252 Asylum St.
Kansas City, Mo.504-7 Railway Ex. Bldg.
Lynn, Mass............48 Lynford Bldg.
New Bedford, Mass..415 Olympia Bldg.
Philadelphia, Pa....710 Widener Bldg.
St. Joseph, Mo......Corby-Forsee Bldg.
St. Louis, Mo..1303 Boatmen's Bk. Bldg.
Sioux City, Ia..427 Grain Exchange Bldg.
Springfield, Mass....217-18 Bowles Bldg.
Worcester, Mass.......212 Slater Bldg.

STEEL REALTY DEVELOPMENT CORPORATION

INTERNATIONAL REALTY DEPARTMENT

Executive Offices, Sixth Floor, Lincoln Bldg., Buffalo, N. Y.

BRANCH OFFICES IN UNITED STATES

Albany, N. Y................32 State St.
Atlanta, Ga.........631 N. Forsythe St.
Brooklyn, N. Y........162 Montague St.
Buffalo, N. Y....6th Floor Lincoln Bldg.
Buffalo, N. Y..........1320 Hertel Ave.
Buffalo, N. Y.........390 So. Park Ave.
Chicago, Ill...........405 Mallers Bldg.
Cleveland, O..........344 Hanna Bldg.
Denver, Col.....405 Guardian Tr. Bldg.
Harrisburg, Pa..........303 Yoffee Bldg.
Lakewood, Ohio.....1395 Brockley Ave.
Lockport, N. Y.............Clinton Bldg.
Louisville, Ky.........1210 Starks Bldg.
Milwaukee, Wis.406 Railway Exch. Bldg.
Newark, N. J............128 Market St.
New York City, N. Y....152 W. 42d. St.
Pittsburgh, Pa...........325 Fifth Ave.
Rochester, N. Y......100 Cornwall Bldg.
Seattle, Wash........220 Douglas Bldg.
Spokane, Wash..506 Spokane S. & L. Bldg.
Syracuse, N. Y.......406 Herald Bldg.
Utica, N. Y..........320 Kempf Bldg.
Yonkers, N. Y.....203 Whitehouse Bldg.

BRANCH OFFICES IN CANADA

Executive Offices, 304 Royal Bank Bldg. Toronto, Ont.

Brantford, Ont.............12 Queen St.
Edmonton, Alta..........10106 101st St.
Hamilton, Ont.......437 King St., East.
Hamilton, Ont............220 Ottawa St.
London, Ont......307 Royal Bank Bldg.
Montreal, Que..612 Dominion Exp. Bldg.
Montreal, Que......421 Mt. Royal, East.
Ottawa, Ont..................Jackson Bldg.
Toronto, Ont......305 Royal Bank Bldg.
Toronto, Ont......2078 Gerrard St., E.
Toronto, Ont..........1632 Dufferin St.
Vancouver, B. C.........431 Richards St.
Victoria, B. C...............644 Fort St.
Windsor, Ont....17-18 Royal Bank Bldg.
Winnipeg, Man.604 Merchants Bank Bldg.

19. Locations in 1922 (*Steel Sparks,* November 25, 1922)

Later that evening, as the group was finishing dinner at the nearby Lafayette Hotel, Steel appeared again: "A pleasant surprise to all was the unexpected appearance of Mr. Steel in the dining room at the hotel just as the members of the party were finishing dinner. Mr. Steel had made a special trip downtown just to tell 'the boys' the substance of news of wonderful business done in Steel Chain Stores that had been received by him since his morning visit."

It is easy to understand why his employees loved him. They thought they were building the world's greatest retail empire.

2

The Creative Promise of the L. R. Steel Company

Ten Thousand Lollipops

L. R.'S BIG IDEA was not his only idea. This energetic visionary was full of ideas, many of them good. But he was not just a visionary; he actually implemented many of his ideas in the company. His creativity was evident throughout his enterprise. Reading the newsletters reveals a company that was way ahead of its time in many ways, and Steelites were frequently aware of it.

His creative marketing ideas included early implementations of two techniques that are common today: the loss-leader concept and the use of charity to enhance corporate visibility in the community. His biggest marketing idea, turning Niagara Falls into a permanent exposition and center of world commerce under the Steel's brand, was well beyond his ability to implement, but that fact did not keep him from trying.

He also was an early adopter of business-structure concepts that have subsequently been successful at major corporations. He was not the first person to recognize the power of vertical integration to control the entire supply chain, but he certainly made an extreme attempt to implement it by going so far as to purchase a coal mine as a secure energy foundation for the enterprise. He also anticipated Sam Walton's insight that he would rather be the only store in a small town than one of many in a larger community. Perhaps the most creative concept was to design a store that placed the shopper in a home furnished entirely with products available at Steel's. You can see a modern implementation of this idea at IKEA.

Social trends were undergoing fundamental changes in the 1920s, and he tried to integrate these changes into his business practices. Greater freedom and independence for women resulted in management positions as well as experiments with scantily clad lingerie models. He also provided employment for the elderly and handicapped, although his opportunities for blacks were still restricted by the common stereotypes of the day.

Marketing Ideas

L. R. discovered that corporate charity was good for business. His early experience giving away sandwiches to soldiers as they arrived at the train station taught him a valuable lesson that he used consistently.

On Christmas Day 1921, he rented Lowes Theater in Buffalo to provide a free movie and gifts to twenty-five hundred poor children.

There was also an annual summer outing for poor children. On Tuesday, August 29, 1922, he arranged an outing to Erie Beach on the Canadian shore. The children were encouraged to bring their parents, and ten thousand lollipops were distributed. Any modern advertising person would

DID THEY HAVE A BIG TIME? THE PICTURE TELLS

Scene in front of Loew's Theater, Buffalo, on Christmas morning following the free entertainment given for poor children, each child receiving a bag of gifts upon leaving. The little chap inset at the left is using the horn he found in his gift bag to give vent to his joy.

20. Free movie for poor children (*Steel Sparks*, December 31, 1921)

make sure that the entire world saw the photo of the kids who won the pie-eating contest held during that outing.

Charity was not just for the kids. Steel's Cafeteria at 297 Washington in Buffalo provided free Christmas dinners in 1921 for two hundred former servicemen who were down on their luck.

In 1921 a severe flood damaged Pueblo, Colorado. L. R. asked his employees to contribute, and they raised more than eight thousand dollars, which was sent to the relief fund on July 9, 1921. Of course, Steel's had a branch office in Pueblo, but the contributions came from all over the country. In that week's newsletter, L. R. said, "I want to congratulate and thank my loyal co-workers in the House of Steel for their fine response to the appeal to aid the Pueblo flood victims. Their efforts have been instrumental in extending a real service of humanity to these people who had their homes swept away. I look upon this accomplishment as another demonstration of the fact that the workers in our organization can always be depended upon in a worthy cause. I am proud of them" (*Steel Sparks*, July 9, 1921).

A photo from the Aurora, Illinois, store shows the implementation of another creative marketing technique. The display shows items being sold at cost. Eggs, sugar, and cans of pork and beans were available here at Steel's cost, but the exact mix of items changed daily. It drew a crowd of buyers who probably stayed around to buy other items. People today recognize this tactic as the loss-leader concept: an item is advertised at a

21. The winners of the pie-eating contest (*Steel Sparks*, September 2, 1922)

EX-SERVICE MEN CHRISTMAS GUESTS OF THE HOUSE OF STEEL

Scene in the Steel Cafeteria in Buffalo when Christmas dinner was served to 200 former service men, who otherwise might have gone hungry. Similar events occurred in the Pittsburgh and Syracuse cafeterias.

22. Free Christmas dinner (*Steel Sparks,* December 31, 1921)

low price to draw traffic into the store. *Merriam-Webster's Dictionary* cites the origin of the term in 1917.

L. R. did not use that term, and it would be difficult to prove that his was the first public implementation of this marketing strategy. He was at least an early adopter of this now common practice. It is interesting to note that the marketing technique would not work well if the same set of items was always available at cost. That predictability would allow shoppers to come in for just those items. The changing mix of items is what drew in shoppers who were likely to buy other items. L. R. got it right.

No one ever accused L. R. of thinking small or lacking vision. A good example of the sweeping scope of his imagination was his plan to turn Niagara Falls into a permanent world's fair that would be *the* center of international commerce. World's fairs were good, but temporary. His plan would have built two hundred buildings at the site and made it a permanent place for the manufacturers of the world to display their wares to the buyers of the world. The buildings would include hotels, auditoriums, sports stadia, an airport, and a railway station.

STEEL STORES REDUCE H. C. OF L.

A view of a section of the grocery department in the L. R. Steel Company, Inc., store at Aurora, Ill., where, at the direction of President Steel, there has been put in operation a unique merchandising plan that helps the thrifty housewife in solving the problem of living costs. The signs shown on the base of this counter tell the story of the plan, each day a variety of goods being placed on sale at cost. As the picture shows, the articles sold at cost on the day this picture was taken were canned pork and beans, eggs and sugar, standard household food requisites. The great volume of business done at this counter is evidence of the public's appreciation of this money-saving opportunity.

23. The loss-leader concept (*Steel Sparks*, February 11, 1922)

He announced it in 1922 and said that he planned to open in 1926, the three-hundredth anniversary of the discovery of the falls. The initial estimate called for spending one hundred million dollars on construction. It was to be developed and managed by the Steel Realty Development Corporation. The minor detail that he did not actually own Niagara Falls was not thought to be a problem.

Always eager to throw a good party, L. R. announced the idea at a large gathering of dignitaries at Marguerite Manor on Friday, October 13,

1922. The event included a tennis exhibition, daredevil flying stunts in an airplane at treetop level, lunch, dinner, dancing, and a lot of speeches. In fact, they made a point of scheduling exactly thirteen speakers just to show that superstition over Friday the thirteenth was not a worry. There were fifteen hundred people in attendance, but they prepared two thousand chicken dinners from the ample supply at his nearby chicken farm. Music was provided by, literally, a "band" of Indians, that is, the Seneca Indian Band from the Tonawanda Indian Reservation at Akron, New York, with the musicians being attired in their tribal regalia.

The keynote speaker was Sir James A. Lougheed, formerly minister of the interior of Canada. He said he was struck with the importance and far-reaching effect of the exposition and declared himself particularly delighted because it was private initiative that projected the big vision. "Looking back," said Sir James, "we see that most progress has been due to the individual. Invariably every age finds some individual, towering above his fellow men like a Colossus. Such a man is Leonard R. Steel. I know of no man who has done as much, not only for Buffalo, but for my country as well" (*Steel Sparks*, October 21, 1922).

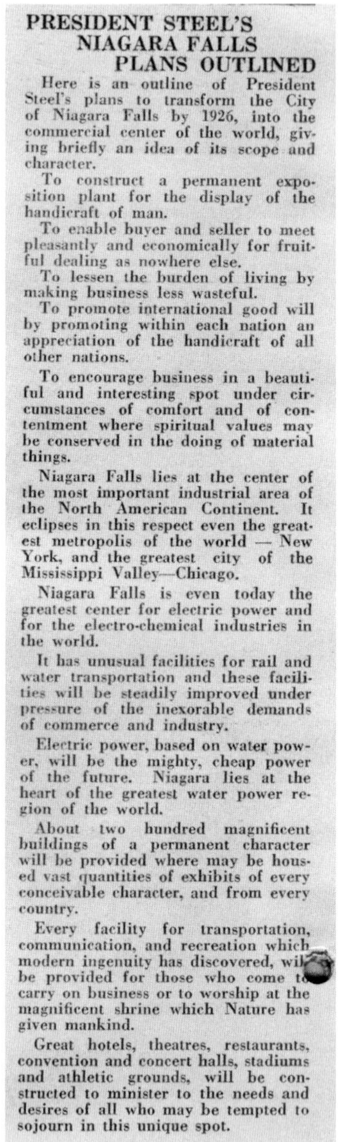

PRESIDENT STEEL'S NIAGARA FALLS PLANS OUTLINED

Here is an outline of President Steel's plans to transform the City of Niagara Falls by 1926, into the commercial center of the world, giving briefly an idea of its scope and character.

To construct a permanent exposition plant for the display of the handicraft of man.

To enable buyer and seller to meet pleasantly and economically for fruitful dealing as nowhere else.

To lessen the burden of living by making business less wasteful.

To promote international good will by promoting within each nation an appreciation of the handicraft of all other nations.

To encourage business in a beautiful and interesting spot under circumstances of comfort and of contentment where spiritual values may be conserved in the doing of material things.

Niagara Falls lies at the center of the most important industrial area of the North American Continent. It eclipses in this respect even the greatest metropolis of the world — New York, and the greatest city of the Mississippi Valley—Chicago.

Niagara Falls is even today the greatest center for electric power and for the electro-chemical industries in the world.

It has unusual facilities for rail and water transportation and these facilities will be steadily improved under pressure of the inexorable demands of commerce and industry.

Electric power, based on water power, will be the mighty, cheap power of the future. Niagara lies at the heart of the greatest water power region of the world.

About two hundred magnificent buildings of a permanent character will be provided where may be housed vast quantities of exhibits of every conceivable character, and from every country.

Every facility for transportation, communication, and recreation which modern ingenuity has discovered, will be provided for those who come to carry on business or to worship at the magnificent shrine which Nature has given mankind.

Great hotels, theatres, restaurants, convention and concert halls, stadiums and athletic grounds, will be constructed to minister to the needs and desires of all who may be tempted to sojourn in this unique spot.

24. Niagara Falls plans (*Steel Sparks*, October 21, 1922)

The idea was inspired, and L. R. might have made it work if he had time. Buffalo would have become the center of world commerce. However, by October 1922, he was only a couple of months away from being forced

25. A band of Indians (*Steel Sparks,* July 15, 1922)

to resign. On the other hand, he did have time to give his idea a name, the Niagara Falls Exposition Company, Ltd., and he may have actually sold some stock in it.

The world really could have used the permanent international clearinghouse for commerce and culture that he envisioned; that goal is now best embodied in the Internet. Niagara Falls was never developed as a center of international trade, but it was seriously considered for the headquarters of the United Nations in 1945 before New York City was selected.

Business-Structure Ideas

L. R. started with the five-and-dime stores and then added the "service" division to sell stock in them. Then he started a real estate and development company to buy and remodel the retail locations he was opening. He wanted a string of candy stores near or in his other stores, so he opened Mary Lincoln Candy. Rather than buy expensive sugar to make the candy, he bought an entire sugar-production facility in Florida, the Moore Haven Division. He added two cafeteria chains, his own Steel's Cafeteria and one that he purchased, Weeghman's. Then he started the Farms Division to provide wholesome food for the cafeterias, even turning Marguerite Manor on Getzville Road into a chicken farm as a demonstration of his commitment. There was also a separate string of lingerie, waist, and hat shops, as these items were best sold in their own environment. Eventually, he wanted to build factories to manufacture the goods for the five-and-dime stores, but he never got quite that far.

This network of twenty or more companies, all doing business with each other and dependent on the others' survival and performance, with money and stock trails tangled among them all, certainly seemed suspicious to the authorities in 1923, but it might look quite familiar to a modern Japanese executive. The concept of *keiretsu,* a set of companies with interlocking business relationships and shareholdings that essentially creates its own protected ecosystem, is often cited as an important factor in Japan's postwar economic miracle. L. R.'s implementation may not have been flawless, but the idea had merit.

L. R. realized that his vast enterprise would need a consistent supply of the most basic ingredient in any operation, energy, so he bought six thousand acres of coal land in Montgomery County, Virginia. "Steel Industries are now assured of an adequate coal supply no matter what degree of uncertainty as to fuel conditions may confront the Americanadian nations from time to time" (*Steel Sparks,* September 2, 1922). Production was 150 tons per day, but could be raised to 1,500 tons per day with investments in new equipment. Coal from this mine had been one of the chief sources for the Confederacy during the Civil War and had, in fact, actually powered the Confederate ironclad *Merrimac* in its famous battle with the *Monitor.*

The coal was to be sold on the open market, but L. R. pointed out that in an emergency, he would organize preferential deliveries for his shareholders (now up to fifty-five thousand), his employees, and his stores. How many people in 1922 were making serious plans for energy independence?

L. R. knew a good market when he saw one, but he never finished his plan of putting a store in every city with more than five thousand people. His idea was to become the only retail outlet in small towns by offering almost everything that people needed for their daily lives and keeping prices so low that competitors were discouraged.

> Rapid progress is being made in the development of the project through which our chain of 700 combination department stores and model markets will be opened throughout the United States and Canada. Our plans call for the establishment of these stores in every city of 5,000 or more population in every state in the union and every province in the

> dominion. Within a very short time, work will be started on the construction of these stores, and it is proposed to have the first of them in operation by June 1, next.
>
> A unique plan that assures the greatest economy in operation has been adopted for the management of these stores. Each will be of standard construction to be built on our own property. The stores will be operated on a group system with one store, part of which will be a warehouse, as the distributing center of merchandise required in six other stores within a radius that insures easy access. A general manager of each group-unit will have headquarters at the central store. (*Steel Sparks*, February 4, 1922)

That idea was left for Sam Walton to work on.

As the company grew, L. R. decided to move upmarket to larger stores with a wider variety of items, including higher-priced merchandise. He wanted customers to be able to buy almost everything needed in their homes from a single store. To present this concept dramatically to the public, L. R. built an entire small house inside his corporate headquarters at the Lincoln Building in Buffalo. It was furnished entirely with items available from Steel's. The idea of the homelike setting was to make it easy for people to imagine the products in their own homes while in a comfortable setting. This idea was very popular, and visitors lined up to see the bungalow, as reported in the July 15, 1922, newsletter:

> Chief interest seemed to center upon the pretty inviting bungalow that had been built in a corner of the spacious second floor. Complete in every detail, this little house, with its parlor, dining room, two bed rooms, kitchen and bath, constitutes a most striking and impressive demonstration of the realization of President Steel's aim to provide comfortable homes and their requirements for the people of moderate means.
>
> The bungalow is furnished complete throughout, not the slightest detail having been overlooked. It constitutes an example of such a home as anyone would be proud to call his own.
>
> And, what is of most interest and greatest concern, is the fact that this little home has been furnished throughout with the goods obtainable in Steel's Department Stores, with no article in its complete furnishings

THE HOUSE THAT STEEL BUILT AND FURNISHED

This is a view of the exterior of the attractive bungalow, which, completely furnished with goods obtainable in Steel's Department Stores, was one of the chief features of the exhibition in the Lincoln Building, Buffalo, arranged for the gathering of executives and managers held on July 8, 9 and 10.

26. "The House That Steel Built and Furnished" (*Steel Sparks,* July 15, 1922)

> costing in excess of $20. In the years to come, as Steel Service is extended to all the people, many similar homes will be found in all parts of the North American continent.

It is hard to say if L. R. was the first person to use this merchandising concept, but he was at least early. If you have ever been to an IKEA store, it is easy to see that it is still popular today. As they say on their website, they hope to "inspire people with realistic room settings and real-life homes" (Inter IKEA Systems B.V. 2011).

Social Trends

A revolt against the accepted Victorian attitudes toward women began with the end of the Great War. Women's independence was symbolized by shorter dresses and bobbed hair. They had won the right to vote in 1920, and new labor-saving devices, such as the electric iron, were freeing them from some of the traditional drudgery of housework. They shopped for clothes and cosmetics at Steel's, but they also worked there in great numbers.

MORE WOMEN IN STEEL SERVICE WIN PROMOTION

More promotions in recognition of accomplishments in the field are announced this week by General Supt. A. J. Todd. Again women play an important part in these promotions, further demonstrating that in Steel Service the field of opportunity is just as broad for women as for men.

Mrs. B. McPherson, one of the "Busy B's" in Mrs. Borden's division in the Greater New York office, has been promoted to managership and assigned to have charge of the office in Brooklyn. What Mrs. McPherson has done in the past is the best evidence of what may be expected from her in the future.

Two women members of the Salesforce in the downtown office in New York also come in for promotions. Mrs. Rose A. Johnstone has been appointed assistant manager of the Brooklyn office, while Miss Sara Furman has been appointed assistant manager of the branch office at No. 165 Broadway, New York City. Their choice for these positions, of course, is based on their proven ability and they are certain to add greater accomplishments to their records in their new assignments.

Another member of the Knickerbocker Office staff in New York has been advanced to managership. He is George L. Curren, formerly assistant manager of Division D, who has been named manager of Division A. Mr. Curren is a live wire and the results of his energy are certain to be reflected in big things from Division A.

The executive personnel of the Greater Pittsburgh office is strengthened by two other appointments. E. S. Bowen, formerly a member of the Pittsburgh salesforce, has been made assistant manager of Division D, while H. W. Pheasant, formerly a member of the sales staff in the Altoona office, has been appointed assistant manager of Division A in Pittsburgh. Both are hard workers and will prove valuable aides in their new work.

A WINNING "FARMERETTE"

Miss Monica Schalk, assistant manager of the Buffalo office of the Farm Division, who led the division in production for the week ended April 22, and holds the distinction of securing the largest individual contract reported in the division to date. Miss Schalk, who formerly held a clerical position in the Buffalo executive offices, is proving the fine opportuntiy open for women in Steel Service.

27. (*left*) Promotion of women (*Steel Sparks,* November 4, 1922)
28. (*right*) From secretary to salesperson (*Steel Sparks,* May 6, 1922)

L. R.'s company, especially his sales force, was a meritocracy; people who did well advanced, and those employees who did not left. In many cases, women prospered in this environment, and they were promoted into management positions. It was not unusual for young women to move into sales from a clerical position. Steel was creating an empire from scratch, not protecting an "old boys'" network, so performance took precedence over gender.

Mrs. Ethel McParlin of Buffalo was a good example. She went from the strong start praised in a company article on June 12, 1920, to being the manager of a new branch office. When she died suddenly in September 1921, the Steelites collected funds to provide for the education of her thirteen-year-old daughter, Margery. On the first anniversary of her death in September 1922, the company remembered her with flowers for her grave in Hartland Central Cemetery, near the home of her parents in Barker, New York. It was that kind of a place. If Steel's had still been in business

BUFFALO SALES WOMAN DOES SPLENDID WORK

Mrs. Ethel McParlin

Manager Stevens of the Buffalo branch office has a real saleswoman in the person of Mrs. Ethel McParlin. Mrs. McParlin joined the sales force three weeks ago. The first week she produced twelve shares, the second week nine shares and the third week thirty-six shares. She is a plugger every minute and promises to be one of the top-notch producers in the campaign for "a Million in June."

29. An excellent start (*Steel Sparks,* June 12, 1920)

A SPLENDID BEGINNING

We want you all to know Miss Ethel Wright who is proving herelf more than Wright (right)—a Steelite—by bringing in production the first week after initiation. Two new partners for the House of Steel through Division C, better known as the "Crimson Ramblers," can be credited to Miss Wright.

Miss Wright is a College graduate, a former teacher, Business College graduate and just finished ten years' service as Department Head of a large New York Publishing House previous to coming into Steel Service.

We are anticipating speedy results and substantial returns from Miss Wright's executive and general ability, and we are extending congratulations on her good start.

30. Bad timing (*Steel Sparks,* February 3, 1923)

by the second anniversary of Ethel's death, there probably would have been more flowers.

Perhaps we should also be reminded that there are no guarantees for women, or anyone else, in business. Poor Ethel Wright, with a college education and good professional experience, got off to a good start with Steel's about a month before the company went bankrupt.

Not all of his ideas worked as intended, but that fact did not keep them from appearing in the newsletters. For example, he tried using live models, chosen from the staff, to model corsets and lingerie. The sales clerks walking around in their undies attracted a crowd, but produced some unexpected results.

The article started out by pointing that it was an innovative event. "A unique innovation in the display of women's intimate wear was inaugurated in the Steel Lingerie, Waist and Hat Shops in Quincy, Ill., and Ottumwa, Iowa, recently by F. E. Hochreiter of the specialty shop executive staff, when there were held live model exhibitions of corsets and lingerie. It was the first time any such exhibitions had ever been given in these cities and they were attended by large crowds of women."

However, the article ends with this remarkable paragraph: "It is interesting to note that among the first to purchase corsets in the Quincy

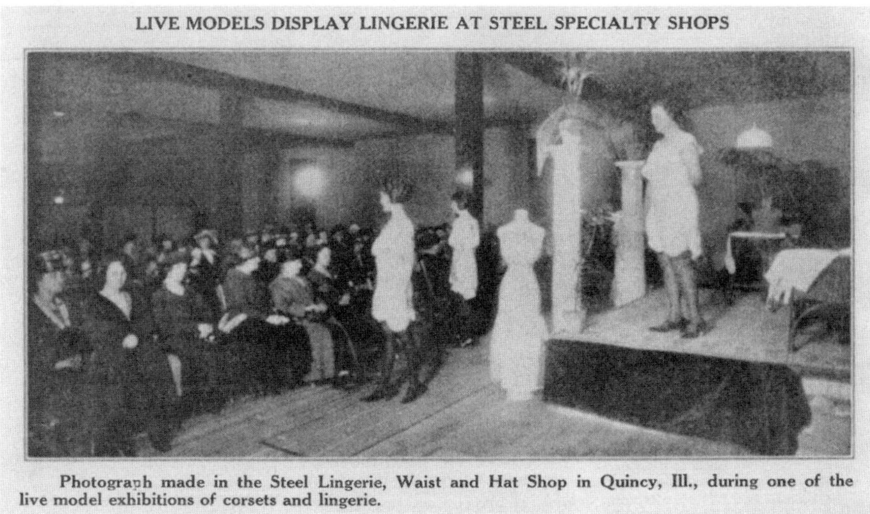

LIVE MODELS DISPLAY LINGERIE AT STEEL SPECIALTY SHOPS

Photograph made in the Steel Lingerie, Waist and Hat Shop in Quincy, Ill., during one of the live model exhibitions of corsets and lingerie.

31. Live models (*Steel Sparks,* April 2, 1921)

store was Alfred DeMero, the famous female impersonator, whose figure, obtained by the use of corsets, has been the envy of women admirers" (*Steel Sparks*, April 2, 1921). There was no mention if the live-model experiment was repeated, but it could not have been tried at all in Victorian times.

Steel's was also open to employing nontraditional workers who were handicapped or elderly. Elmer Calvin of Cincinnati was clearly older than his coworkers, but an article on February 3, 1923, mentions only his consistent success. On the other hand, the eightieth birthday of George Rich of the Salt Lake City office was celebrated with pride. Here is a fellow who stays young because he loves his work.

FULL OF CONFIDENCE

Here is a likeness of Elmer P. Calvin, Division B, Cincinnati. Mr. Calvin is one of the most consistent producers working out of the Cincinnati office, and every Steelite should meet him. Mr. Calvin's contention is that he has not yet found the person who will refuse him an interview. He has the stick-to-it-iveness that puts it across.

32. Elmer P. Calvin (*Steel Sparks*, February 3, 1923)

CELEBRATES 80TH BIRTHDAY

George W. Rich

George W. Rich, one of the salesmen of the Salt Lake City office has just celebrated his eightieth birthday. Mr. Rich is a fine old gentleman, who has kept himself young by his association with the House of Steel. He thoroughly enjoys his work, and says the only thing he regrets is that the days are not long enough.

33. George W. Rich (*Steel Sparks*, October 14, 1922)

You might expect George Rich to be the oldest employee, but that prize goes to John Thompson, a happy eighty-three-year-old salesman in the Toronto office who has an attractive young lady on each arm in one photo. The copy under the cheery photo reveals something even more interesting: these young ladies are not relatives or secretaries—they are managers from neighboring Steel's offices. Clearly, Steel's was a different kind of company.

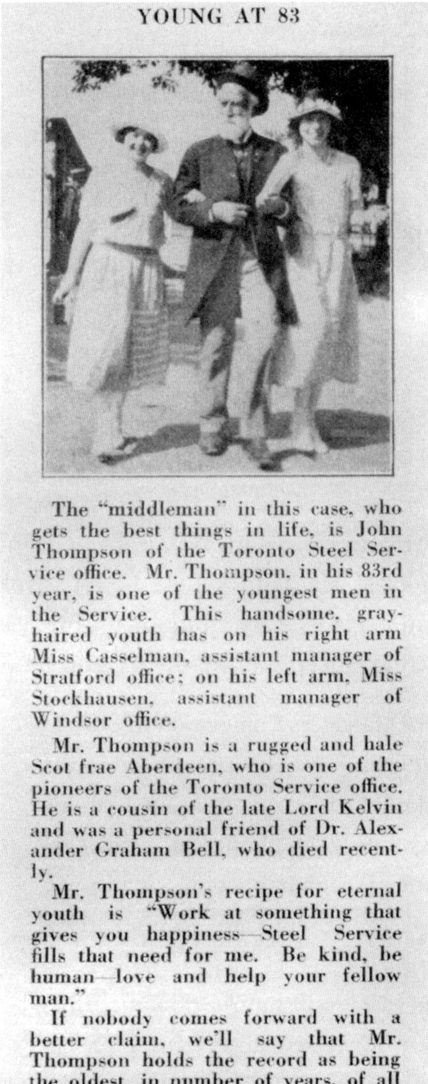

YOUNG AT 83

The "middleman" in this case, who gets the best things in life, is John Thompson of the Toronto Steel Service office. Mr. Thompson, in his 83rd year, is one of the youngest men in the Service. This handsome, gray-haired youth has on his right arm Miss Casselman, assistant manager of Stratford office; on his left arm, Miss Stockhausen, assistant manager of Windsor office.

Mr. Thompson is a rugged and hale Scot frae Aberdeen, who is one of the pioneers of the Toronto Service office. He is a cousin of the late Lord Kelvin and was a personal friend of Dr. Alexander Graham Bell, who died recently.

Mr. Thompson's recipe for eternal youth is "Work at something that gives you happiness—Steel Service fills that need for me. Be kind, be human—love and help your fellow man."

If nobody comes forward with a better claim, we'll say that Mr. Thompson holds the record as being the oldest, in number of years, of all Steelites in the organization, working daily on System Street.

34. The oldest employee (*Steel Sparks*, August 12, 1922)

Poor E. J. Kershner probably dreaded job interviews more than most people. He may have had difficulty gaining employment anywhere else, but he was a successful dry-goods buyer for Steel's. His photo appears in the newsletter, and the article makes no reference to the obviously disfiguring growth on his face. It is probably a cavernous angioma that usually forms before birth or shortly after and is a form of birthmark. It is not cancerous but would have been dangerous to remove back then owing to the risks of excessive bleeding and the large area of scarring. Modern reconstructive surgery could have taken care of it, but with some difficulty (Dr. Harold Griffin, personal communication, July 24, 2009).

Steel's did not have any black salespeople or managers, but they

35. E. J. Kershner (*Steel Sparks,* February 26, 1921)

did use a black employee in an advertising campaign. "Doughnut Dan" worked in a Chicago cafeteria at 169 West Madison, where he was well known by the customers for his big smile. He was also famous for his "24-karat, 12-cylinder, joy-packed, rib-tickling, succulent, super-doughnuts."

> During the big Steel Service and Store Managers Convention in Buffalo in July, a large advertising stand, cut from heavy board, was set in the Weeghman display, showing "Doughnut Dan" larger than life with his marvelous smile and a tray of doughnuts. "Doughnut Dan" appealed strongly to President Steel and Charles Weeghman: consequently, Mr. Weeghman will have large stands of "Doughnut Dan" in his various restaurants from coast to coast.
>
> It is quite likely that "Doughnut Dan" will figure prominently in the Weeghman advertising campaign in newspapers, perhaps later in street cars and on posters, until Weeghman's "Doughnut Dan" becomes one of the most famous advertising characters in America. (*Steel Sparks,* August 5, 1922)

36. Doughnut Dan (*Steel Sparks,* August 5, 1922)

Doughnut Dan is cast from the same mold as other stereotypical black advertising characters of the day such as Aunt Jemima and Uncle Ben. The opportunities open to women at the start of the 1920s were not yet available to blacks. In the same year that women won the right to vote, total membership in the Ku Klux Klan was estimated at 4.5 million people (Allen 1931, 57). On racial issues, L. R. was not the pioneer that he was in other areas.

L. R. did draw some early criticism from people in the investment community. One analyst (*United States Investor* 1921, 30) was uncomfortable with the financial details in the first annual report. There were eight separate entities combined under one corporation, which made it difficult to track the financial relationships among them. Goodwill accounted for one-quarter of the value of the company's assets, an unusually high percentage. Also, this analyst questioned the source of funds used to pay the thirty-eight thousand dollars' worth of dividends, as no profits were

37. Doughnut Dan advertisement (*Steel Sparks*, October 7, 1922)

reported. Finally, there were large expenses for office furniture and Persian carpets.

These details did not trouble L. R., though. He always had one more big idea to excite him. It is easy to imagine him saying, "But wait, there's more!"

3

Inventing the Infomercial

Fifty Endings

LEONARD RAMBLER STEEL came of age along with the motion picture industry. His birth in 1878 was almost coincidental with a technical insight that demonstrated the possibility of motion pictures.

In 1877 Leland Stanford, then governor of California, had made a casual bet with a friend over whether a horse ever has all four hooves off the ground at the same time while running. Stanford was sure that the horse was airborne at some point, although it was hard to determine from normal observation. He decided that it ought to be possible to take a photo of a horse at exactly the right time to prove his point.

Stanford hired Eadweard J. Muybridge, a well-known photographer, to take that exact photograph. Muybridge soon recognized the difficulty of this project but applied some ingenuity to solve it. He used a series of cameras in a row to shoot a succession of photos. The shutters were tripped at just the right time as the horse encountered threads attached to them. This idea worked, and he was able to pull out the exact photo to prove Stanford's point.

The unintended consequence was the recognition that a series of photos, when looked at in rapid succession, provided the visual impression of a moving image. Modern films run at twenty-four frames per second to provide smooth, continuous motion, but even at slower speeds, the novelty of a choppy moving image had instant appeal.

Muybridge recognized a business opportunity and developed a machine that he called a Zoopraxiscope to project moving images on a screen from a series of photographs on a rotating disk. This device allowed him to go on the lecture circuit to present scientific studies of various animals and people in motion. In the interest of science, and perhaps commerce, the images sometimes included naked women.

The highlight of Muybridge's career came in 1893 when he lectured on the science of animal locomotion at the Columbian Exposition in Chicago. He used his Zoopraxiscope to show moving pictures to an audience who had paid admission, making this event the first commercial showing of a movie. L. R. would have been fifteen at the time and was probably not aware that a new industry had begun.

As we have seen frequently in the computer industry, the first innovation is not always a commercial success. Unfortunately for Muybridge, Thomas Edison was also interested in motion pictures. A series of cameras was replaced with a single camera that could take a series of pictures, and the spinning disk was surpassed by the more flexible medium of continuous film. Edison's first commercial product, the Kinetograph, allowed silent movies to be shown to a single viewer at a time. The commercial and aesthetic limitations of this format were obvious, and Edison soon was projecting a single image on a screen to an audience as Muybridge had successfully demonstrated in 1893.

Starting in 1896, movie houses began to emerge as a new form of entertainment showing the novelty of people and objects in motion. Early films were often shown along with a Vaudeville stage show, but they soon replaced the live performers entirely. The movies allowed the performer to be seen in many locations while being paid for only one performance, so they rapidly became a low-cost form of mass entertainment. Also, they had the good fortune to have a ten-year head start over the next innovation that would provide even cheaper entertainment, namely, radio. L. R. would have been in his early twenties when he saw his first movie, and it probably cost him a nickel.

Up until 1915, movies were usually short one- or two-reelers that did not need much of a plot. The novelty of motion was enough to draw an audience. There were acrobats, dancers, chase scenes, travelogues, and comedies. The actors were usually nameless, and the directors were basically camera operators. Even without a star system, movies expanded rapidly. The industry matured suddenly in 1915 with the release of *Birth of a Nation.* This twelve-reel, three-hour film was both an artistic and a commercial success, despite its controversial racial content, and had a lasting influence on the industry. Lillian Gish became a star, and D. W. Griffith became a star director. Plots, emotions, and dramatic tension became more important to audiences than mere movement. Feature-length films became more popular than the shorts, and the cost of admission went up. L. R. probably saw *Birth of a Nation* when it came out. At the age of thirty-seven, he would have been successful enough to afford the increased admission of two dollars.

Just as an energetic businessperson growing up in the Internet era would want his own website, L. R. wanted his own movie. But he did not want to be in the entertainment industry; his insight was to use a movie to sell stock in his business. It was only a matter of time until someone invented the infomercial. Ron Popeil, gadget inventor and late-night television pitchman, can claim only second place.

WONDER PICTURE SHOWN IN HARRISBURG

The Orpheum Theatre, Harrisburg, Pa., as it appeared during the showing there this week of "Pennsylvania Hills to the Chain of Steel Industries."

38. Picture shown in Harrisburg (*Steel Sparks*, March 25, 1922)

Without any false modesty, L. R. called his film "the greatest industrial picture ever shown on the North American continent." He created a three-hour silent film about his life and his company. The title was *Pennsylvania Hills to the Chain of Steel Industries.*

The film opens in Middletown, Pennsylvania, the small town where he was born, chronicles his rise from country boy to manager of a chain of seventy-four stores, and closes with the idea that he would rather deal with ordinary people than the rich bankers on Wall Street. Of course, it was shown for free.

It was his marketing genius at its best. A team of advance men would go to a town, rent a movie theater, place some ads in the local paper, and hire a band to play in front of the theater. Sometimes, free food was included if the crowd looked like it might be less than full capacity. The free tickets were printed in the local newspaper; all you needed to do was sign your name and address on the ticket. If L. R. had lived in the computer age, he would have invented cookies. Of course, these free admission coupons went directly to the sales force. I think we can see how L. R. sold stock to sixty thousand people.

A forty-eight-page pamphlet was distributed to the audience. It referred to some scenes in the movie but did not just repeat the plot. Instead, it provided more detail about L. R.'s family history and business success. In case someone missed the message from

39. Free pass to the movie (*Manitoba Free Press*, July 19, 1922)

the movie, the pamphlet summed it up clearly: "The story of industrial development, seen in Pennsylvania Hills to the Chain of Steel Industries and elaborated in this book which you have read, portrays how the Small Investors of the World may combine their savings under the leadership of sincere, honest, experienced men and directly realize that earning power which their money should enjoy" (Gifford 1922, 48).

Genesis of the Idea

L. R.'s first interest in movies was mentioned in the May 14, 1921, newsletter. He said that the "movie man" would be visiting every branch office and every store to create a film that would be shown at the second annual convention in Buffalo. The convention was held from October 10 to October 13, and the movie, as promised, was ready. It was shown on Tuesday evening at the Broadway Auditorium, the biggest hall in the city.

Steelites attending the convention marched through the business district to the auditorium accompanied by music from three bands. They marched with flags, banners, and flaming torches. There was ample cheering for President Steel, who was waiting for them inside.

The general public had been invited, and about five thousand showed up for a six-reel presentation that showed the interiors and exteriors of many of Steel's offices and stores around North America. Gerald K. Rudulph, who later became an agent in Hollywood, narrated as the audience cheered and yelled.

L. R. may not have been sure that the movie, by itself, would be sufficient for an evening's entertainment, so he followed the showing with an exhibition of Indian club juggling by Emil Rouy, a talented Steelite from the Paterson, New Jersey, office. L. R. always wanted to make sure that everyone went home happy.

The enthusiastic response from the audience at the convention must have helped him see the mass-marketing potential of movies. L. R. was probably also influenced by propaganda films made by the Committee on Public Information, a government agency that tried to direct public opinion in favor of entering World War I. *The Kaiser, the Beast of Berlin,* staring Lon Chaney Sr., was a big hit in early 1918. It made an emotional appeal, like L. R.'s film, but there was no attempt to get the audience to buy anything. The coordinated stock-selling campaign based on the leads generated by the free movie tickets is the element of originality that distinguishes L. R.'s film from mere advertising or propaganda.

Perhaps another influence on L. R. came from a brief five-minute film by Charlie Chaplin called *The Bond.* In this self-produced film from 1918, Chaplin makes an overt appeal for people to buy Liberty Bonds. This plea is closer to L. R.'s intention, but it did not have the associated sales campaign that was enabled by the registration for the free showing.

In fact, L. R.'s sales campaign had the look and feel of the drive to sell Liberty Bonds during World War I. Music and patriotic fervor were a big part of both campaigns. There were also flags, banners, heroic art, and a lot of big meetings. The volunteer army of seventy-five thousand "Four-Minute Men" may have been a prototype for L. R.'s sales force. These amateur orators were encouraged to give brief patriotic speeches about the virtues of Liberty Bonds to any audience they could find. Movie intermissions were a favorite target.

Was L. R.'s film really the first infomercial? Until somebody produces an earlier example, I will bet on L. R. An infomercial is not just mass marketing or advertising; it is entertainment with an embedded advertising message, along with some mechanism for the customer to execute an order. The late-night television shows have an 800 number to call; L. R. had his sales force to call on viewers.

Big Crowds

In the November 21, 1921, newsletter, L. R. hinted at his idea. He stressed that his salespeople were really educators, not just salespeople, "for you are in truth educating the people in the manner of securing the greatest return from their money safely invested. I have given much thought and time to perfecting plans for a campaign of education. . . . Within a short time the details of this plan of education will be announced. The plan is unique. It will bring us before the people as no other method could."

The official announcement by L. R. came in the January 28, 1922, edition of *Steel Sparks:*

> Final details are now being worked out in perfection of a campaign of publicity and education that I am sure will be of great value and importance in carrying out the programme of expansion of our organization. This is the plan to which I made reference in a previous article in "Steel Sparks," it now having progressed to the point where I am able to reveal definitely its nature.
>
> This publicity-educational campaign has the form of a motion picture exhibition which will give a comprehensive visual resume' of the important events and accomplishments of our organization, from the birth of the idea on which it is founded to the present time. About the first of March sets of these motion pictures will be ready for public exhibition.
>
> It is our purpose to show these vivid pictorial records of our enterprises in cities and towns throughout the United States and Canada and their exhibition is certain to create in the public an interest that will result in mutual benefit to our organization and those who, through this means, are aroused to accept the opportunity of becoming co-partners in our vast, ever-growing business.

Pennsylvania Hills to the Chain of Steel Industries opened simultaneously in three cities on March 13, 1922. One was Middletown, Pennsylvania, because he never forgot his hometown. Another was Toronto, because he always made sure that the Canadian operations were included as equal partners. The third first-day showing was in Denver, because L. R. and Marguerite were there for the groundbreaking on his next big project. About a thousand people had to be turned away from the first showing in Denver, as the theater was at capacity. Standing-room only was the normal course of events. In Montreal fifteen thousand people, including the mayor, saw it in one week.

L. R. made fifty copies of the ten-reel film so that it could circulate easily. He estimated that it was seen by thirty thousand people every week for at least six months. The film was shown in dozens of cities throughout North America in 1922. I do not have a complete list of showings, but here are some of the cities mentioned in the newsletter:

40. Capacity crowd at showing (*Steel Sparks,* April 1, 1922)

Akron, Ohio
Allentown, Pennsylvania
Baltimore, Maryland
Boston, Massachusetts
Brantford, Ontario
Buffalo, New York
Cincinnati, Ohio
Columbus, Ohio
Davenport, Iowa
Dubuque, Iowa
Hanover, Pennsylvania
Hartford, Connecticut
Kitchener, Ontario
Lawrence, Kansas
Erie, Pennsylvania
Montreal, Quebec
New Bedford, Massachusetts
New Haven, Connecticut
Ogden, Utah
Owen Sound, Ontario
Paterson, New Jersey
Sault Ste. Marie, Michigan
Seattle, Washington
Sioux City, Iowa
Sturgeon Bay, Wisconsin
Troy, New York
Vancouver, British Columbia
Wheeling, West Virginia
Wilmington, Delaware

Outline of the Film

The movie took eight months to make and three hours to show. Silent films were normally accompanied by a person on a piano or organ.

L. R. used a six-piece orchestra in some, if not all, of the showings. Cutting corners was not in his nature, especially when he had a good idea. Besides, he had a lot of competition. Stars like Hoot Gibson, Mary Pickford, Buster Keaton, and Rudolph Valentino all released films in 1922. The blockbuster film of the year was *Robin Hood,* with Douglas Fairbanks.

Harry J. Sprang was the cinematographer who took most of the film, and he sometimes showed up as the projectionist. Edward Cochems, who was manager of the motion picture department, sometimes gave an introductory talk. He was caught up in the patriotic fervor when he said, "In it you will see the 4,000 Steelites marching north, south, east, and west to make living conditions better for humanity through the genius and master mind of Leonard R. Steel" (*Steel Sparks,* February 18, 1922).

No stock was sold at the showings. L. R. wanted to make sure that people felt comfortable and did not feel any pressure. He knew that his sales force would be visiting in person in the next few days.

I have certainly not seen the film, but I have read enough reviews that I have been able to reconstruct the general outline in some detail. Here, more or less in order, is what the viewers saw:

- opening scene: his birthplace in the Pennsylvania hills, Middletown
- L. R. as a child "playing store"
- L. R. as a child in a country school
- his first job sweeping out a country store
- riding twenty miles each way on the train every day to get to his next job
- L. R. leaves home for his first job in "big business"
- L. R. praying at the graves of his parents
- launching his own business in Buffalo
- scenes of the executive offices in Buffalo
- scenes of the Canadian headquarters in Toronto
- scenes from the sales convention in Buffalo, showing the large size of the sales force
- scenes of convention attendees (who all paid their own expenses) visiting Niagara Falls

- aerial views of Niagara Falls from both the American and the Canadian sides
- scenes of a reception at L. R.'s farm
- scenes of jubilation in the sales office over the first sale of stock in the Farm Produce Stores Corporation (the chicken farm that was located at L. R.'s country home)
- it was announced that it would take two hours to show all the retail stores, but quite a few were shown, both inside and out
- scenes from the Steel Realty Development Corporation
- scenes from a Steel Cafeteria
- scenes from a farm owned by the Farm Produce Stores Corporation that supplied the Steel Cafeteria
- the Mary Lincoln Candy factory
- the Moore Haven Sugar Corporation in Florida, supplier to the candy factory
- scenes of Steelites distributing five hundred baskets of free food to needy families at Christmas
- scenes of stock trading on Wall Street with the subtitle that L. R. could hold his own with the titans of industry, but preferred to be with the common people
- the climax comes when the film announces that the L. R. Steel Company will be opening an office at (insert the name of a major local office building) so that the local people could become partners in the enterprise

The final reel of the ten-reel movie was customized for the locality where it was shown. Audiences were thrilled, even after three hours, to actually see their local office or store (or the future store location). It was an exceptional touch that made people feel as though they were already a part of this wonderful company. In some cases, local people were waiting for the Steel office to open on the morning after the movie. They were thrilled to be able to buy stock in the company. L. R. had correctly anticipated the appeal of localization in advertising. This movie was not just the first infomercial; it was also a very effective one.

Does a copy of the film still exist? Is there still a copy of the movie around? He made fifty copies . . . Are they all gone?

The very last showing was in Buffalo for the district attorney's office as part of a fraud investigation. By then, all the free showings around the country would have stopped; the bands were gone, and there were no salespeople around to follow up on the leads. The film may be in an evidence storage unit somewhere in Buffalo, but all my attempts to find it were in vain. There were no records of it, and they certainly were not going to let me in to rummage around in the area where they store evidence. Even if it was found, it probably would have been badly deteriorated by now.

Since the business collapsed quickly, some copies may have been left at the movie houses. They would have had no reason to keep them, but sometimes people do things for no good reason. I got very lucky in finding the newsletters; it might happen again.

On the other hand, many early movies were recycled to recover their silver content, so the scrap value of the copies may have ensured their destruction.

L. R.'s film is not the only one to be lost over time. Of the 525 films released in 1921, only 50 are known today (Everson 1998, 14).

4

The Life of a Salesman at the L. R. Steel Company

"How's Yer Pep?"

"STEELITES" COULD BE FOUND ANYWHERE; churches, theaters, restaurants, and, of course, at your doorstep. They gave people the opportunity to become part of a cheerful organization by owning shares in Steel's. These "Steelites" were the heirs of the Liberty Bond Four-Minute Men who approached strangers with patriotic zeal. The difference, now, was that they made a lot of money, if they were successful.

Some words from back then have gone out of fashion today—for example, *pep, dandy, swell,* and *jolly*—but they seemed to fit well in the early stages of the Roaring Twenties. They were frequently used both by and about the salesmen at Steel's. They were sincere people who honestly believed they were introducing their customers to a wonderful opportunity. In retrospect, they now seem very innocent.

The Salespeople

"Wanted: Four men possessing initiative and executive ability. You can learn of a rare opening to engage in steady employment. Advancement steady and sure. If you are ambitious to get on in the business world, apply in person. But don't apply unless you are willing to work" (advertisement in the *Trenton Evening News,* April 3, 1921). People from many backgrounds answered this type of ad to become salespeople for Steel's. There were probably around five thousand salespeople and managers, at most, but if you consider that there was a lot of turnover, the total number of people who worked in sales during Steel's existence was much higher.

The sales organization did not include the people who worked as sales clerks in the stores. These people were in a separate division. The salespeople at Steel's sold stock, or, more precisely, contracts for stock, as

41. Full of pep (*Steel Sparks*, March 11, 1922)

INCORPORATED UNDER THE LAWS OF THE STATE OF DELAWARE.

10242

L. R. STEEL COMPANY, INC.

AUTHORIZED CAPITAL

$10,000,000 PREFERRED STOCK PAR VALUE $100. PER SHARE — 100,000 SHARES OF COMMON STOCK WITHOUT NOMINAL OR PAR VALUE.

This is to Certify that MRS. NELLIE HOLLIFIELD, is the owner of THREE shares of the COMMON STOCK of L. R. Steel Company, Inc. transferable in person or by attorney upon the surrender of this certificate duly endorsed. A statement of the rights, privileges, preferences and voting powers and of the limitations and restrictions of the preferred stock is printed upon the back hereof, and this certificate and the shares represented hereby are issued and shall be held subject thereto and to all the provisions of the Certificate of Incorporation and the By-laws of the Corporation, copies of which are on file at the office of the Corporation.

In Witness Whereof the company has caused this certificate to be signed by its duly authorized officers and its corporate seal to be hereto affixed, this day of DEC 10 1920

THE EQUITABLE TRUST COMPANY OF NEW YORK

THE CORPORATION TRUST COMPANY NEW YORK

42. Stock certificate

most people financed the purchase through a convenient payment plan offered by the salesperson.

I have noted previously that Steel's provided many opportunities for women. For example, young Monica Schalk of Buffalo was able to rise from a clerical position to become assistant manager of a sales office. But there were also opportunities for more mature women like Mrs. F. H. James of Rochester, who was a leading producer. Few salespeople of either gender could probably match the determined stare of Miss Katherine Prescott of the Boston office.

43. Mrs. F. H. James (*Steel Sparks,* April 22, 1922)

44. Katherine Prescott (*Steel Sparks,* November 4, 1922)

Many of the men had military backgrounds and submitted photos of themselves in the uniforms they wore in the Great War. Young Ernest Ash of Halifax, Nova Scotia, survived the war and started a sales career at Steel's in 1921. So did H. W. Pheasant of Altoona, Pennsylvania. Warren F. Lawrence started in the Boston office at about the same time. His more aggressive looks may have been influenced by his experience in the aerial service in France during the war. The camaraderie and spirit of the military provided a good background for life at Steel's.

Of course, salespeople came from other backgrounds, too. E. G. Clarke of Peterboro, Ontario, was one of the many teachers who were tempted into sales. Big George Earnst of the Albany, New York, office still looks like he is capable of returning to his former profession; he was a cop.

I mentioned the oldest salesperson in chapter 2, but there was also a youngest salesperson. Emanuel J. Grober of the Albany, New York, office was only eighteen but already a star performer.

45. Ernest Ash of Halifax, Nova Scotia (*Steel Sparks,* March 26, 1921)

46. H. W. Pheasant of Altoona, Pennsylvania (*Steel Sparks,* April 1, 1922)

47. Warren F. Lawrence (*Steel Sparks,* January 15, 1921)

As in most organizations, particularly sales organizations, there were a few characters. One of my favorites is Lucile Michaels of the Spokane, Washington, office. Her friends called her "Spokannie," and she was known for her western brand of pep. And, yes, I do think that she has a

48. E. G. Clarke of Peterboro, Ontario (*Steel Sparks,* April 1, 1922)

49. George Earnst of Pittsburgh, Pennsylvania (*Steel Sparks,* April 16, 1921)

50. Emanuel J. Grober of Albany, New York (*Steel Sparks,* December 4, 1920)

bull whip in her left hand. There was a Mutt-and-Jeff combo in the Pittsburgh office. The big fellow is Emile Schroeder, the office manager, and the shorter one is his assistant, H. M. Pheasant. And there was a father-son combo in New York City. Herman Reiss was so successful that he convinced his son Louis to join the company.

Clockwise from above: 51. Lucile Michaels of Spokane, Washington (*Steel Sparks,* October 8, 1921)
52. Mutt and Jeff (*Steel Sparks,* December 30, 1922)
53. Herman and Louis Reiss of New York City (*Steel Sparks,* September 30, 1922)

I have not found any African American salespeople; it would have been too much to expect for even such an open company as Steel's. Steel's did have at least one Hispanic salesperson, Jose Garcia Rios of the New York City office.

As in any organization, there were a few people with unusual or unfortunate names, such as Miss Annis Groo of the New York City office. Stewart Ellsworth Queer, a former minister from Buffalo who decided to try his luck at sales, would probably change his name if he was around today.

54. Jose Garcia Rios of New York City (*Steel Sparks,* May 20, 1922)

55. Annis Groo of New York City (*Steel Sparks,* June 24, 1922)

56. Stewart E. Queer of Buffalo, New York (*Steel Sparks,* March 11, 1922)

57. Chief Elijah Menass of London, Ontario (*Steel Sparks,* December 9, 1922)

And, finally, L. R. proudly reported that an actual Indian chief was a member of the sales force. Chief Elijah Menass of the London, Ontario, office carried the good news about Steel's stock to his people on the Sarnia Reserve.

The System

L. R.'s approach to selling stock in his companies was grounded in the firm belief that the salesperson was providing a valuable service to the client. That conviction is why he called his sales organization the L. R. Steel *Service* Company.

The customers were not just part of the organization; they actually owned the various Steel companies. The newsletters were an internal method of communicating with a sales force spread over the United States and Canada, but they were also available to the customers. Not many contemporary companies would be comfortable sharing detailed sales techniques, strategies, and results with their customers, but Steel's was a different kind of company. L. R. had nothing to hide. The motto on the newsletter's logo was "Honesty, Loyalty, Truth," and he took it seriously.

I used to work for a company that tried to improve the civility of its meetings by asking people to behave as though customers were present. This rule probably produced more levity than civility, but it was considered to be an enlightened approach, and the company was frequently rated as one of the best places in America to work. L. R. was in good company.

58. "The Way Is Open to All" (*Steel Sparks,* February 25, 1922)

L. R. tried to be a micromanager, which must have been frustrating for his far-flung sales force. He was very confident in his system, as this quote from the August 20, 1921, newsletter shows: "There is only one way to sell a prospective client, and that is to adhere strictly to the Steel system of selling. Follow that system to the letter and you will succeed."

There was a sales meeting every morning. These meetings seem to have been more motivational than content oriented. The goal was to leave the office with a lot of pep.

Every salesperson went through a training phase that involved learning the "sales talk." The exact text of the sales talk does not appear in the newsletters, but it certainly must have focused on the opportunity to profit from being an owner in this rapidly growing business. I am sure there were some specific phrases that were supposed to work like magic; the goal was probably to give the salesperson an extra bit of confidence.

59. Honesty, Loyalty, and Truth (*Steel Sparks*, April 1, 1922)

L. R. devised a sales aid containing a set of photos of his prominent business locations. Here are his instructions for using it with the sales talk:

> The photographs show properties in the best locations in the different cities. Placed in front of a client, accompanied by comprehensive explanations, the folders in themselves and the word picture of the salesman or sales woman should make a profound impression. The first folder, properly placed on a client's desk or table, should excite his interest. The second should increase that interest. The third should bring forth an expression of wonderment and the fourth should sell him.
>
> Facts are facts, and when backed up by something a man or woman can see, those facts will stand the test of any negative argument. We had these folders printed because we believed your clients should see what they are buying. As a clincher to your sales talk, these folders speak volumes. (*Steel Sparks*, February 12, 1921)

Miss Margery Lysaght is presented as proof that the magic works. This stenographer-turned-salesperson started bringing in business for the Newark office as soon as she learned her sales talk.

After learning the sales talk, salespeople were encouraged to give it to prospects at least ten times a day. Like the patriotic "Four-Minute Men" of the Liberty Bond drive, they were encouraged to approach strangers in crowds or go door-to-door looking for people who might buy stock in one of L. R.'s companies. L. R. was convinced of the value of making ten calls per day:

> Among the many offices in our service organizations you will find men and women who produce consistently. How do they do it, you ask? I will tell you. Because the consistent producer is filled with that brand of enthusiasm that finds its source in the overmastering conviction that he is engaged in a work that is of real value and importance to mankind. He backs up his enthusiasm by work. His enthusiasm is enduring and he teams it up with at least all that is demanded from headquarters in this organization, and that is: "TEN CALLS A DAY." (*Steel Sparks*, March 26, 1921)

Where did they get enough time to make all those calls? Well, part of the system seems to have been limiting lunch to just twenty minutes.

60. Margery Lysaght (*Steel Sparks*, February 5, 1921)

61. "Ten Calls a Day" (*Steel Sparks*, November 4, 1922)

The sales were consummated on a one-page document called a "subscription agreement." One share of preferred stock was one hundred dollars, but they were encouraged to buy two and get a free bonus of one share of common stock. A 7 percent dividend was promised. A deposit was required, but the customer could make monthly payments and receive the colorful stock certificates when the full amount was paid. After the subscription agreement was turned in to the local Steel's office, the customer would get a letter from the sales manager, congratulating him or her for a wise decision.

Activities

Salespeople at Steel's were used to many group activities. They were encouraged to think of themselves as part of a successful company that enhanced their self-image. They were all Steelites, and it was a source of pride.

62. Your identity (*Steel Sparks,* October 28, 1922)

Each salesperson was also a member of an office team that played endless games of fantasy baseball based on sales production. Recent scores and rankings were updated in every issue of the newsletter. Each team had a snappy name like the Spokane Speeds, the Buffalo Originals, the Pittsburgh Panthers, or, unfortunately, the Tacoma Wood Ticks. The competition was mild and good-natured because, in the end, they were all Steelites. They partied together and often scheduled events on holidays. It was more than a job; Steelites belonged to a jolly group of people who had a swell time together.

On December 31, 1920, the Seattle Steel's sales organization had a banquet for forty-four people in the Blue Room of the Washington Hotel. Western district manager Will Hahn, who attended, described it this way: "It was a little gem—one of those scintillating, inspiring affairs that makes a fellow just tingle with pep" (*Steel Sparks,* January 15, 1921).

There were songs, balloons, humorous impersonations, a piano solo, and presentation of a gold watch to the highest producer, triggering a

63. New Year's Eve in Seattle (*Steel Sparks,* January 15, 1921)

"splendid" acceptance speech. Hahn, as a visiting executive, was given two gifts. One was a small totem pole carved from walrus tusks, and the other was a tall wooden totem pole carved to be an exact replica of the tribal totem pole still standing in Pioneer Square. After midnight, they went to the hotel lobby for dancing with the other guests. I bet they all had a dandy time.

Banquets were held frequently, and, in many cases, the attendees are photographed wearing funny hats that seem to be made of paper. They did not explain the reason behind this odd custom in the newsletters, but I assume it was some sort of group-spirit effort. The photo of a banquet at the Hotel Onondaga in Syracuse was taken on May 29, 1920. They had not yet opened a store in Syracuse when the photo was taken, but then every good business venture should start out with a banquet funded by the company.

Surprise parties were also so common that we must wonder if the element of surprise was diminished. The "surprised" executive would be lured somewhere on his birthday to find a roomful of his coworkers singing. Secretary-treasurer Fred Dobmeier was the subject of such a surprise party in Buffalo in September 1920.

> Secretary-Treasurer Fred Dobmeier had a birthday last Wednesday and he thought he would keep it to himself. He succeeded for a time and then something happened. President Steel learned about it first and he

64. Totem pole in Seattle, Washington (photo courtesy of Lorraine Cherry)

> quietly relayed the news to other executives in the Service Corporation and the Stores Company. The result was that Fred was escorted by Editor Rudulph to one of the large dining rooms in the Lafayette Hotel on Friday noon and there he found the entire forces of the executive offices of both the service corporation and the stores company assembled in his honor.
>
> The surprise upon Mr. Dobmeier was complete. When he arose from his seat to respond to a brief talk and presentation of gifts from the service corporation and the stores company, he was quite overcome and it was some minutes before he could gather himself together.

Among his gifts was "something in a silver flask that can not be mentioned because of a possible violation of the Volstead Act" (*Steel Sparks*,

65. Funny hats (*Steel Sparks,* October 7, 1922)

66. At the Syracuse banquet (*Steel Sparks,* June 5, 1920)

October 2, 1920). Upon returning to his office, he found his desk covered with flowers, as expected.

On July 18, 1922, the Syracuse Steelites had a wonderful time driving down to Skaneateles Lake for a banquet at Krebs' Hotel. It was not just employees; the Steelites included friends, family, and customers, too. They were able to form a caravan of automobiles leaving in unison from the office at 433 South Salina Street because a special police detail had

WHEN SECRETARY-TREASURER FRED DOBMEIER HAD A BIRTHDAY

67. Fred Dobmeier's birthday (*Steel Sparks,* October 2, 1920)

68. Krebs' Hotel in Skaneateles, New York (*Steel Sparks,* July 29, 1922)

reserved all the parking places for them. The cars formed a parade with banners and singing passengers as it drove out of town. Enthusiasm, pep, and fraternalism predominated.

Their photo was taken on the porch after a sumptuous meal. The well-fed and probably tired Steelites made it back to the office in time for an evening business meeting where eastern superintendent E. F. Tanner delivered "an unusually instructive address on finance" (*Steel Sparks,* July 29, 1922). We can only imagine how many people nodded off during this address.

The Sales Conventions

The biggest group events were the annual sales conventions. They had the spirit of revival meetings, with a few good meals and some sightseeing thrown in.

The first convention lasted five full days in early October 1920. The 1921 convention was scheduled for four days, but they decided to add a fifth day when they fell behind shchedule. Both were held in Buffalo and had very similar agendas. They voted to hold the 1922 convention in Cleveland, but it never happened. The organization had gotten too large by 1922, so they had a smaller meeting that was limited to the regional managers.

Buffalo's Memorial Hall was packed for the opening day of the first international convention. Steelites, mostly salespeople and managers, came from all over the United States and Canada. The Canadian contingent rented a special train for the trip and brought the Royal Canadian Grenadiers' Band along as their contribution to the entertainment.

Gerald K. Rudulph, the editor of the newsletter, was the master of ceremonies. He introduced Buffalo's acting mayor, Arthur W. Kreinheder, who welcomed the conventioneers; they welcomed him back with a round of "For He's a Jolly Good Fellow."

L. R. was introduced to wild cheers and applause. His brief speech praising the efforts of all the Steelites was interrupted many times by spontaneous enthusiasm. He called almost every executive to the stage for a personal introduction to the crowd. Rudulph eventually broke his gavel while trying to subdue the excited audience.

69. First international convention (*Steel Sparks,* October 9, 1920)

70. Royal Canadian Grenadiers' Band (*Steel Sparks,* October 9, 1920)

The events included a sightseeing trip to Niagara Falls and a dance in the ballroom of the Lafayette Hotel. The banquet for 935 at the Lafayette Hotel was the largest ever held there. Another evening was spent at Shea's Theater, and the Buffalo and Toronto offices held a friendly baseball game.

CONVENTION DELEGATES ENJOY TRIP TO NIAGARA FALLS

One of the many interesting events of convention week was the trip to Niagara Falls, where the above remarkable photograph was made.

71. Convention delegates at Niagara Falls (*Steel Sparks,* October 22, 1921)

At the end of the convention, L. R. and most of the other executives went to the train station to personally thank the Steelites as they were leaving.

Slogans

One of L. R.'s favorite slogans was "I'd rather make men than money." This motto seems to be an odd slogan for a company with so many women in it, but his point was that self-improvement (by being associated with the company) was more important to him than income.

A more interesting one is the one-word slogan THINK, shown in a photo of a meeting in the Detroit office. The same sign appears in several other photos, so it appears to have been in widespread use in the Steel's organization. This sign, especially in all capital letters, is commonly associated with IBM. It was IBM founder Thomas Watson's favorite slogan. This point raises some interesting questions: Who came up with the slogan first? Did one of these early entrepreneurs "borrow" it from the other one?

We know that Thomas Watson lived in Buffalo when he worked for the National Cash Register Corporation, and Steel's was an NCR customer (I have a copy of a letter confirming a large order of cash registers), so the potential for some cross-pollination of ideas exists. The timing favors Watson. He was with NCR from 1895 until 1913, well before Steel's was founded. In 1914 he joined the Computing Tabulating Recording Corporation, the company that he renamed IBM in 1924. Many sources credit Watson with creating the THINK slogan while he was at NCR, so if that is correct, it would have been before Steel's, which was founded in 1919.

72. "THINK" (*Steel Sparks,* March 25, 1922)

One credible source says that Watson's longtime friend Lee Olwell traces the origin of the slogan to a specific frustrating sales meeting at NCR in December 1911. Olwell says Watson asked him to make a placard with the word *THINK* on it because he thought the problem with the sales force was that they did not think enough (Maney 2003, 147).

On the other hand, the slogan was clearly in use at Steel's before IBM was IBM. It is always possible that this situation is an instance of simultaneous independent discovery where two creative people came up with the same idea, much like Newton and Leibniz both inventing calculus at about the same time near the end of the seventeenth century.

At least there is no doubt about the origin of the Steelite song; it was written just for them:

It's always fair weather
When good Steelites get-to-gether,
With contracts on the table
And a good song ringing clear.
(*Steel Sparks,* February 18, 1922)

5

The Stores

The Best Fifty-Cent Chicken Dinner in Canada

THE GOOD THINGS IN LIFE were never more abundant than at the start of the Roaring Twenties in North America. L. R.'s personal calling was to bring this abundance to the average family. Things that would have been unimaginable luxuries in prior days were now "everyday miracles": radios, toasters, washing machines, electric lights. Distributing these articles to the common people at a minimum of cost was the joyous task of Steel's stores.

The abundance of delicate glassware in the well-organized display at the Aurora, Illinois, store must have been as inspirational to the local shoppers as it was to the proud Steelites who took the photo. If any of it has been lucky enough to survive until now, it is probably in an antique collection.

Store interiors were spacious and well lit. There always seemed to be room for a potted palm. The merchandise was out in the open so that customers could handle it and make their decisions in a comfortable environment.

The bright store in Ottumwa, Iowa, had jewelry and other more expensive items in glass cases. The photo was taken on December 4, 1920, just before the customers were let in for the first time.

The merchandise also included many things that were not luxury items. The Quebec City store seems to have a stack of toilet paper prominently displayed at the end of a counter next to the socks and sweaters. Toilet paper came into commercial availability only about forty years before this photo was taken, but it had become a necessity in every home. L. R.'s goal was to have his stores provide 75 percent of the things needed in every home so that customers could do most of their shopping there.

73. Everyday miracles (*Steel Sparks,* February 25, 1922)

74. The store in Rock Island, Illinois (*Steel Sparks,* November 6, 1920)

Grand Openings

New store openings were exciting events for both the Steelites and the local population. There was a party atmosphere, with music, free food, and plenty of Steel's pep. The picture of the grand opening of the Port Jervis, New York, store shows a large crowd of eager shoppers listening

75. The store in Ottumwa, Iowa (*Steel Sparks,* December 11, 1920)

76. Toilet paper in Quebec (*Steel Sparks,* December 24, 1920)

to the band and waiting in line to get into the store. It was taken on September 4, 1921.

Grand openings all seemed to follow the same marketing formula. After the store was finished, stocked, and polished to a shine, there would be a preview, where people were allowed in to look but not to buy. Visitors who attended the preview were given small gifts, typically a flower for the ladies, a cigar for the men, and candy for the kids. The preview helped build demand and ensured that news of the wonderful merchandise available at Steel's would spread through the community.

On opening day, usually a Saturday, a band would be playing in front of the store, and crowds would gather to hear the music. Local police would be hired to do crowd control, a move that was probably rarely seen in most small towns. It helped create the feeling that it was a very special event.

The local mayor was encouraged to give a speech to the crowd, which gave him a chance to praise his town, his constituents, commerce in

AT THE OPENING OF OUR STORE IN PORT JERVIS, N. Y.

Photograph shows a portion of the crowd that streamed into the store from morning until night on September 4.

77. Grand opening in Port Jervis, New York (*Steel Sparks*, September 18, 1920)

general, and Steel's in particular. L. R. attended as many store openings as possible, but if he could not make it, some other executive would be there to give a speech on his behalf.

When the doors finally opened, the crowd would surge in to find that a big grand-opening sale was on. Prices were always surprisingly low, and the excited shoppers shopped.

Later that evening, the mayor would attend a banquet with L. R. (or his stand-in) at the finest hotel in town. There would be another round of speeches praising the local town, commerce in general, and Steel's in particular.

The grand opening of the first Montreal store on January 14, 1921, followed this script almost flawlessly. I say almost, because I expect that opening two weeks after the Christmas shopping season was not part of the original plan. I hope that the fellow in charge of organizing the opening did not get into too much trouble, because that fellow was my great-uncle, Clayton Pickard, my original motivation for investigating the company. When he first appeared in the newsletters only four months previously, he had just been promoted to be in charge of all the American stores after

78. The store in Montreal, Quebec (*Steel Sparks,* January 22, 1921)

working in Canada. Then he was back in Canada, organizing the grand opening for the new store. Subsequently, he is mentioned as a buyer in the Toronto office. The newsletters were always too cheery to carry news of any demotions, but the job he was promoted to must not have worked out.

The big Montreal store, called the finest chain store in North America, was located at 467–475 St. Catherine Street East. It had 86 feet of street frontage and was 160 feet deep, providing a total of more than 25,000 square feet of selling space on the main floor and in the basement. The old building still stands today. It is now the home of a shoe store with big signs in the window saying, "All Shoes Must Go" and "Nous Liquidons Toute Notre Marchandise."

Mayor Medric Martin and his wife were there for the grand opening. They were shareholders, of course. Speaking in French, he praised this "new and greater system of merchandising" that was making its first appearance in Montreal. He said he liked Steel's concept because it would lower the cost of living for the laboring people of Montreal, the people he liked the best. In fact, he recommended that his chauffeur shop there and think of this recommendation as a sort of salary increase. A 25 percent savings at Steel's was just like getting a raise.

79. Inside the Montreal store (*Steel Sparks,* January 22, 1921)

Mayor Martin had a nice tribute for L. R.: "We don't often find a man with the energy and unselfish ideas of Mr. Steel. I believe that he was born to play the role he is playing today. For that reason, I say he is an extraordinary man. I wish you long life that you may finish a wonderful career for good. I am sure God will bless you for trying to do something for your fellow man" (*Steel Sparks,* January 22, 1921). He closed by commenting that he would be back to go shopping with his wife so he could save some money.

L. R. made a brief speech, being careful not to upstage the mayor and mindful of the large crowd of shoppers eager to get at the merchandise. Soon after the doors opened, the store, cafeteria, and soda fountain were packed. The cafeteria in the basement boasted of having the best fifty-cent chicken dinner in Canada, and many of them were sold that day.

The mayor invited L. R. to spend the night at his country home, the same home where he had recently entertained the future king of England. The next evening, January 15, 1921, was the big banquet at the Windsor Hotel. My great-uncle, Clayton, and his wife were there, according to the article in the newsletter. He should be somewhere in the photo, but I do not find him.

The Montreal store opening, with its speeches and banquet, is probably the origin of a small bit of misinformation in my family. When I first started looking for Clayton, I asked my mom and her older sister for any details that might help me. They consistently said that his wife, who was

80. The Montreal banquet (*Steel Sparks,* January 22, 1921)

from Montreal, was the mayor's daughter. The tale of being at a banquet with the mayor of Montreal could easily have morphed into a closer relationship over the years in the minds of two young girls who were five and eight at the time. The banquet took place before Clayton vanished, so my grandmother would still have been in contact with him.

Steel's business grew rapidly. By January 1921 there were 131 locations in operation in North America, including both retail stores and offices to support stock sales. Some of them were built from the ground up, as with the Montreal store, and others were acquired and run under their original names until they could be rebranded as Steel's. For example, on December 4, 1920, L. R. announced the purchase of seven F. E. Nelson stores in the northeastern United States. These five-and-dime stores had been in business for fifteen years, and the plan was to run them under the Nelson name until they could be fully integrated.

The last acquisition was announced on August 26, 1922. It involved the twenty-six pharmacy stores of the Miller-Strong Drug Company. The chain started in Niagara Falls in 1908, and most of the stores were around the Buffalo area. The acquisition was never mentioned again, so it probably did not become a reality.

Cafeterias

The cafeterias were a special project for L. R. because he loved the idea of stocking them with eggs and fresh vegetables from his own farms. After turning his country home into a chicken farm, he proceeded to buy or lease other farms and started a Farms Division to manage them. Of course, his sales force sold stock to fund the Farms Division's activities.

The first cafeteria in Buffalo was opened for public inspection on New Year's Eve 1920. L. R. was there to hand out cigars to the men and flowers to the ladies. Where else would he rather be on New Year's Eve? The location was at the heart of the downtown business district, 297 Washington, right across the street from the Ellicott Square Building. The cafeteria had white glass-topped tables, light-green walls, a cream-colored ceiling, and red- and gray-tile floors. Chicken dinners were the specialty.

Every cafeteria should have its own truck with the name prominently displayed. The cafeteria in Pittsburgh was even grander. With seating for

THE HANDSOME NEW STEEL'S CAFETERIA IN BUFFALO

Attractive exterior of the magnificent eating place at Nos. 297-301 Washington Street, the popularity of which is daily increasing. On the second floor are the offices of the Buffalo branch of the service corporation.

81. The cafeteria in Buffalo (*Steel Sparks,* January 22, 1921)

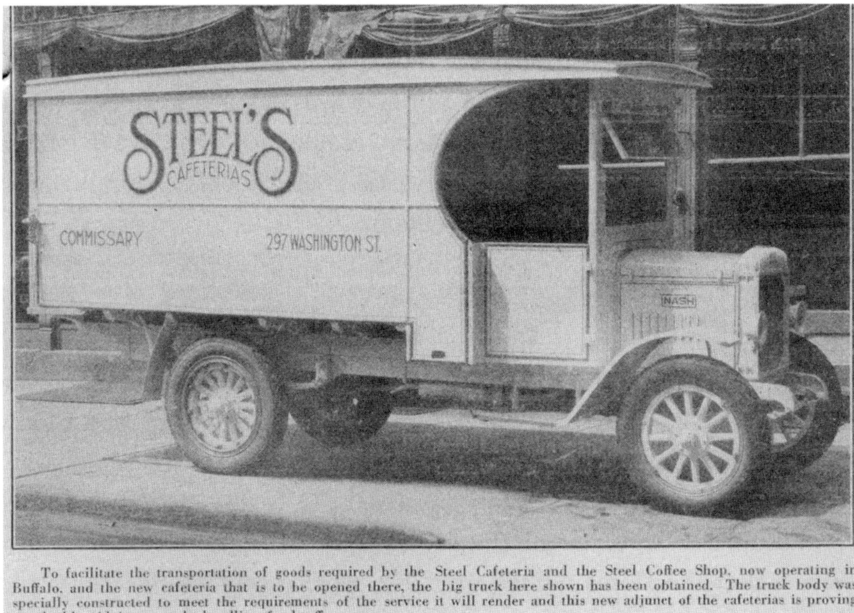

To facilitate the transportation of goods required by the Steel Cafeteria and the Steel Coffee Shop, now operating in Buffalo, and the new cafeteria that is to be opened there, the big truck here shown has been obtained. The truck body was specially constructed to meet the requirements of the service it will render and this new adjunct of the cafeterias is proving a valuable aid in properly handling foodstuffs.

82. The Steel's Cafeteria truck (*Steel Sparks,* August 12, 1922)

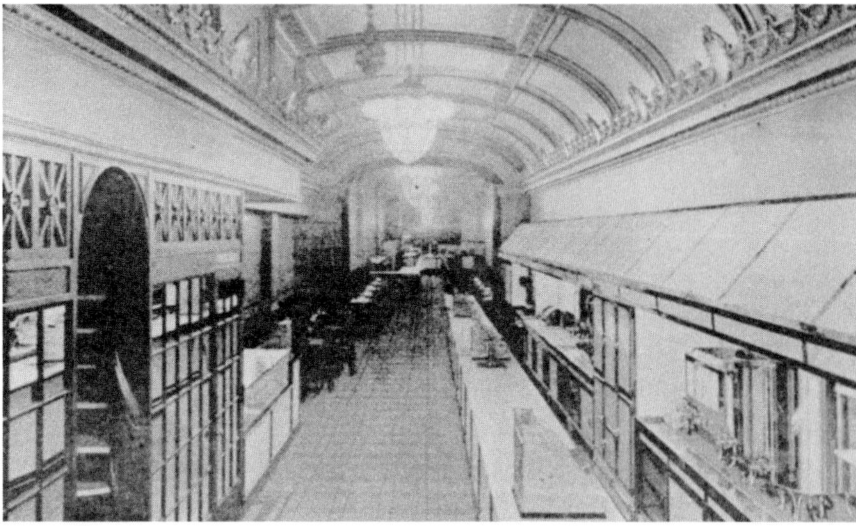

83. Cafeteria in Pittsburgh, Pennsylvania (*Steel Sparks,* December 4, 1920)

seven hundred, it was one of the largest restaurants in the country at that time. It was in a five-story building at 325 Fifth Avenue, and there was a second entrance on Oliver Street, 250 feet away on the other side of the building. Ice-making equipment and cold storage were in the basement, and the bakery was on the top. A full floor was devoted to storage and a laundry equipped with electric washers. Frequently, there was a five-piece orchestra playing on the balcony. A series of elevators and dumbwaiters conveyed people and food between floors.

Candy

The Mary Lincoln Candy shops were also purchased, and the original name was retained. There was no mention of the origin of that name, but in those less legalistic times it was probably easier to just use a highly recognizable name without any official permission. L. R.'s first action after the purchase in 1920 was to reduce prices.

The wife of our sixteenth president was not well known for her cheerfulness, but the stores named after her were exceptionally bright and cheery.

The new Mary Lincoln Candy and Coffee Shop in Lafayette Square Theater and Office Building in Buffalo, which opened on Saturday, March 4.

84. Mary Lincoln Candy (*Steel Sparks,* March 11, 1922)

The interior of the shop presents a scene of beauty. Forcibly impressed upon one on entering is the unusually attractive color scheme, a comingling of white, black and buff, presenting a warm, home-like effect. Beautiful plastic ornaments decorate the panels forming the upper portions of the walls, the woodwork and show-case bases being in white with just sufficient black trim to produce a pleasing effect.

At the left, on entering, is a modern soda fountain completely equipped with the most up-to-date facilities, the fixtures being the embodiment of efficiency, richness, and good taste. Adjoining the soda fountain is a neat appearing light lunch serving counter, under the glass top of which articles that are served are temptingly arranged. The candy counter occupies the entire length of the right hand side of the shop. (*Steel Sparks,* March 11, 1922)

85. Inside a candy store (*Steel Sparks,* July 22, 1922)

In Wilkes-Barre, Pennsylvania, two thousand people were served on the first day that Mary Lincoln was open. Police had to come in to help control the crowds, as usual. Haney Klienkauf's Orchestra was engaged to provide music for the first week of operation just to make sure that things got off to a good start. The tall tables were for people who wanted to stand during a quick snack, and there were booths for people who wanted to take their time.

The Moore Haven Division, a sugar plantation and refinery in Florida, was acquired expressly to provide raw materials for the candy operations. I could find no evidence that sugar from this source was actually used, but the Moore Haven executives attended all the meetings, and the sales force sold stock in their division.

Women's Clothing

Steel's lingerie, waist, and hat shops were L. R.'s venture into the difficult world of women's fashion. Few men are comfortable in that environment, and L. R. was probably as lost as most men would be. However, he plowed forward with his standard approach: low prices (nothing more than ten dollars) and a lot of promotions to pack in the customers. Sometimes these shops were separate stores, but more frequently they were a floor or section of the main retail store.

Here is a good description of a Steel's lingerie, waist, and hat shop that was originally in the March 1921 issue of the *Dry Goods Review* and was reprinted in the April 16, 1921, issue of the newsletter:

> Entering the new shop, which is situated to the left of the huge store, one is impressed by the charm and fine appearance of the fittings and decorations. Against the snowy walls are ranged the solid mahogany show cases alternating with huge mirrors the length of the shop. At the entrance on either side are displayed the lingerie, hosiery and all the numerous dainty accessories of a smart woman's wardrobe. A little farther on are the blouses, which are displayed under glass in the cases and fixtures; and effectively lighted to show up colors and embroideries to the best advantage. All down the center of the floor are placed at intervals pots of handsome ferns, fresh tulips or other spring blossoms, and overhead, swinging among the shallow bowls which shade the electric light into less glaring strength are dozens of cages, each one with its canary singing enthusiastically all day long. No wonder women find it interesting to shop in such surroundings as these, where summer seems to reign all the year around.

Today, music is commonly brought into retail spaces to create the appropriate atmosphere. Again, L. R. was ahead of his time. He had the right idea, and he used canaries to implement it. I know he invented the infomercial, but was he also on the way to inventing Muzak? Maybe the canaries worked, or maybe it was the low prices, but the stores were packed.

Then again, maybe it was the merchandise. "Among the many exquisite novelties displayed one of the most interesting was an imported set of all black Georgette underwear daintily trimmed with gay hand-made fruits in vivid colors" (ibid.).

L. R. was more at home around chicken dinners than ladies' underwear, so it should be no surprise that some of the Steel's lingerie, waist, and

"DOLLAR DAY" SALE DRAWS IMMENSE CROWDS

View of the interior of the L. R. Steel Lingerie, Waist and Hat Shop in Buffalo on Wednesday March 2, showing a portion of the great crowd of shoppers that thronged the store throughout the day eager to take advantage of the bargains offered in the "Dollar Day" sale.

86. Crowds at the Dollar Day sale (*Steel Sparks,* March 5, 1921)

hat shops were eventually transformed into candy stores, soda fountains, and cafeterias.

At the start of 1921, there were 65 Steel's traditional general merchandise stores. There were also 20 cafeterias, 12 candy stores, and 34 lingerie, waist, and hat shops; most of them were combined in the same location with a general merchandise store. The combined revenue from all was expected to be $20 million, and the value of the real estate holdings was estimated to be $6 million.

The New Idea

There was no doubt about the competition; it was the F. W. Woolworth Company. L. R. regularly included

IN OPERATION OR UNDER LEASE BY JANUARY 1, 1921

UNITED STATES

41 FIVE CENTS TO $1 STORES.
18 LINGERIE, WAIST & HAT SHOPS.
12 CAFETERIAS.
7 CANDY SHOPS.

CANADA

24 FIVE CENTS TO $1 STORES.
16 LINGERIE, WAIST & HAT SHOPS.
8 CAFETERIAS.
5 CANDY SHOPS.

131 STORES IN THE UNITED UNITED STATES AND CANADA.

Estimated BUSINESS FOR 1921, $20,000,000.

Value of REAL ESTATE HOLDINGS, $6,000,000.

87. Stores in operation (*Steel Sparks,* December 4, 1920)

Woolworth's sales statistics in the newsletter so that everyone could keep an eye on them and recognize the potential for growth in the chain store business. In 1920 Woolworth's had revenue of $141 million, an 18.2 percent increase over 1919, and they had no debt (*Steel Sparks,* January 8, 1921). They had 1,100 stores, and L. R. wanted to buy them all. The smaller competitors were closer to Steel's size. The S. S. Kresge Company had had 188 stores in 1920, and the W. T. Grant Company had 38 stores in 1920 (Vance and Scott 1994, 4).

L. R. needed a plan to overtake such an established competitor, and he was always ready with a Big Idea. This one was so different that he called it the New Idea.

The idea was originally called the "700 Store Plan" but was soon increased to the "1,600 Store Plan." The idea was to create larger stores, Steel's Department Stores, but put them in smaller towns. They calculated that there were 1,308 towns that had populations between five and twenty

88. "The New Idea" (*Steel Sparks,* July 15, 1922)

thousand. The retail presence in these towns might be old-fashioned general stores or a couple of chain stores. This market was growing increasingly wealthy and was interested in having the retail opportunities of a larger city.

Like many of L. R.'s ideas, it had all the initial appeal of a perpetual-motion machine. A single large store in a small town that supplied almost everything people might want would be the principal, and probably only, retail outlet in the community. It would drive out existing competitors and discourage others just because of its size and range of merchandise. In addition, a chain of 1,600 of them would have enormous buying power, resulting in prices so low that no competitor could possibly compete. Not only could L. R. entirely cut out the middleman, but he could also buy the entire output of some factories and eliminate any marketing expense for the lucky factory. Forty years before Sam Walton opened his first Wal-Mart Discount City in Rogers, Arkansas, the idea of large discount stores in small towns was already alive and well in L. R. Steel.

Large department stores were not a new idea. They have been around since just after the Civil War. Macy's in New York, Wanamaker's in Philadelphia, Marshall Field in Chicago, and Hudson's in Detroit were all well-established businesses when L. R. was making his plans. However, these stores were not discounters. They catered to wealthy people in large cities. L. R. set his sights on a much larger market. He estimated that his total market should be around twenty million people, assuming that some rural residents near the small towns would come to town to shop.

Like the perpetual-motion machine that I "invented" when I was ten, the idea just needed a little push to get it started. L. R. knew that the best way to give his plan a push was to call a big meeting. He called for five hundred executives and managers to come to Buffalo in July 1922 for a three-day meeting. The best hotels, like the nearby Lafayette Hotel, were filled with Steelites. L. R. rented two additional floors just below his corporate headquarters in the Lincoln Building so that he could show them a prototype of his New Idea.

The amazed visitors saw that an entire bungalow had been built on the second floor of this downtown office building, and it had been completely furnished with items available at Steel's, with nothing costing more than

THE HOUSE THAT STEEL BUILT AND FURNISHED

This is a view of the exterior of the attractive bungalow, which, completely furnished with goods obtainable in Steel's Department Stores, was one of the chief features of the exhibition in the Lincoln Building, Buffalo, arranged for the gathering of executives and managers held on July 8, 9 and 10.

89. The Steel House (*Steel Sparks,* July 15, 1922)

twenty dollars, except of course the automobiles. Look closely at the photo of the bungalow. There is an automobile on the left side of the photo, next to the bungalow. Part of L. R.'s plan was to sell a "special type of automobile" that would be available only at Steel's. The car in the photo looks suspiciously like a Ford Model T; it was probably just the demonstration model.

The meeting had the usual round of banquets, speeches, and a visit to L. R.'s country home, where the visitors were surprised to find one hundred thousand chickens and hundreds of ducks.

The stores would carry enough merchandise to supply the normal needs of everyone in the growing middle class: men's and women's clothing and shoes, furniture and other household items, fresh fruits and vegetables, meat and sausage, and eggs fresh from Steel's Farms Division. The stores themselves would all be built to a standard design in order to speed construction and lower costs. Continental Construction, a Steel's company, would build them on land that was owned by Steel's Real Estate division. Everything would be done in-house, if possible.

Stores would be developed in clusters of seven locations that would be managed by a single person. The central store would also have a warehouse and distribution center attached to it. This warehouse would supply the central store and the six branches. The plan was for each branch to be restocked once a week, so seven stores in a cluster seemed appropriate so that one day a week could be devoted to each store. This structure would improve turnover and also create an organization that could be managed by one person.

A new corporation would be set up in each state for this new enterprise, and all the capital raised in the state would stay in that state. There would be plenty of opportunities for Steel's sales force to introduce people to the investment potential of the company.

Because L. R. was both a visionary and a practical person, he started implementing his idea. And guess what . . . he almost made it work.

6

The Denver Miracle

"Meet Me at Steel's Corner"

L. R.'S PERPETUAL-MOTION MACHINE just needed a little push to get started. Once in motion, it would generate enough energy (cash) to keep going under its own power.

The Denver store at the northwest corner of Sixteenth and Welton was the final embodiment of his retail theory. He built a store large enough to dominate a market with low prices and surrounded it with satellite stores that were fed from the same warehouse. The product selection was so wide that there would be little need to shop elsewhere. Low prices and high turnover would keep competitors out, keep customers loyal, and keep investors happy. More stores would mean more opportunities for his employees to grow with the company. It was all going to work, and L. R. was a hero to all.

Financing

In the past, stock sales or bank loans had funded the purchase of existing stores and the building of new ones. But L. R. liked to do everything "in-house" with his own internal resources, which is why he had a sugar plantation for his candy stores, chicken farms for his cafeterias, and a coal mine to power the whole enterprise.

Borrowing money from outsiders must have pained him. Why not borrow from himself? Better yet, why not let his well-paid employees fund the New Idea? It would be the "Steelites' Own Store." The money from the employees was referred to as "subscriptions." The details of the subscription were not discussed in the newsletters, but it is likely that it was done on the same model that was used to sell stock to investors. Investors were asked for a down payment of 40 percent of the price of the stock. The remainder was spread out in equal payments over ten months with no interest added. After the last payment, the stock certificates were mailed to them.

What did the employees get for their "subscription"? It did not seem to be a stock sale. Employees frequently bought stock in the company; they were encouraged to do so, just as they were at Enron. But this situation appears to have been different. I think L. R. simply paid them well and asked them to return some of the money as a donation to build a store.

The subscription campaign opened at corporate headquarters on August 31, 1921, and $60,000 was subscribed in minutes. The names of the sixty-four people who subscribed immediately were published in the next newsletter. My great-uncle, Clayton Pickard, was not listed, perhaps a sign that he was not destined for success with the company. Within a week, they had $112,100 and eventually hit the $300,000 goal. At that time, they had four thousand employees, so a $75 contribution from each of them would have been sufficient to reach the goal.

It was a time when anything was possible. The financing plan worked. They gave him the money. It was hard for anyone to say no to the boss, especially one as well loved as L. R. Steel.

In the September 3, 1921, edition of the newsletter, L. R. wrote, "Words fail me in my desire to express the gratification I feel over the wonderful response already received in the campaign to build and equip our Denver store through the subscriptions of the 4,000

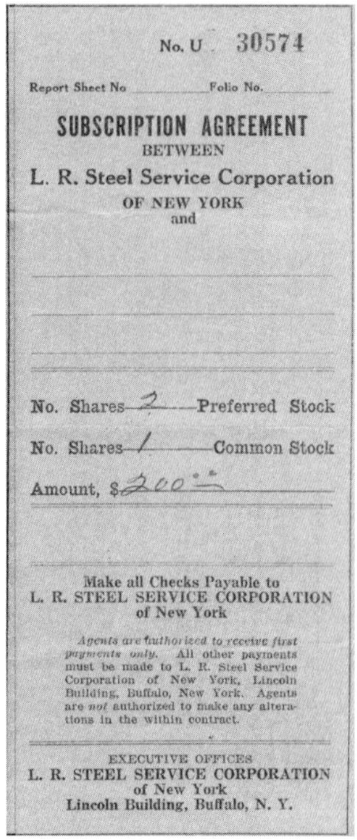

No. U 30574

Report Sheet No ______ Folio No. ______

SUBSCRIPTION AGREEMENT
BETWEEN
L. R. Steel Service Corporation
OF NEW YORK
and

No. Shares 2 Preferred Stock
No. Shares 1 Common Stock
Amount, $200.00

Make all Checks Payable to
L. R. STEEL SERVICE CORPORATION
of New York

Agents are authorized to receive first payments only. All other payments must be made to L. R. Steel Service Corporation of New York, Lincoln Building, Buffalo, New York. Agents are *not* authorized to make any alterations in the within contract.

EXECUTIVE OFFICES
L. R. STEEL SERVICE CORPORATION
of New York
Lincoln Building, Buffalo, N. Y.

90. Subscription agreement for stock sales (author's collection)

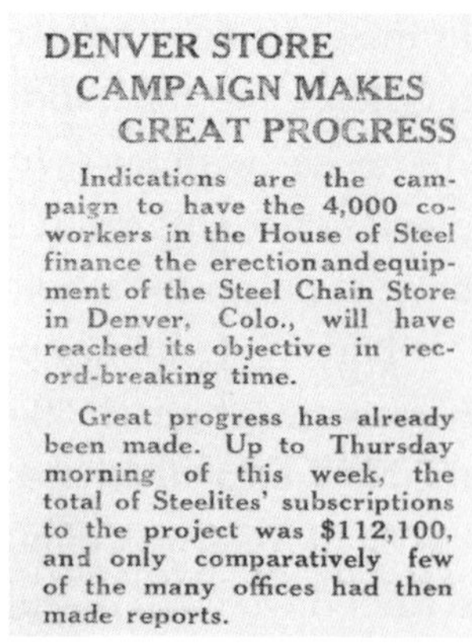

DENVER STORE CAMPAIGN MAKES GREAT PROGRESS

Indications are the campaign to have the 4,000 co-workers in the House of Steel finance the erection and equipment of the Steel Chain Store in Denver, Colo., will have reached its objective in record-breaking time.

Great progress has already been made. Up to Thursday morning of this week, the total of Steelites' subscriptions to the project was $112,100, and only comparatively few of the many offices had then made reports.

91. Denver campaign progress (*Steel Sparks*, September 10, 1921)

workers in the House of Steel. Not only will this Denver store bring financial returns, but it will stand as a monument to those who are working for the ultimate objective, the greatest chain store system in the world."

Background

L. R. loved to travel so he could meet his employees in person and get a feeling for opportunities to expand. He went through Denver in late 1920 as part of a swing through several western cities. Denver was the headquarters for the western district, and the salespeople operated out of a rented office in the Guardian Trust Building.

Will Hahn was the western district manager and L. R.'s close friend. L. R.'s confidence in him was probably a major factor in the decision to build in Denver. Will had a tragic air about him after his young wife passed away suddenly in 1921 while on a business trip with him in Seattle. Will was one of L. R.'s favorites before his wife's death, but L. R. was even more fond of him afterward. He wanted Will to be successful and treated him as though he were a younger brother. This close relationship was perhaps

92. Will Hahn (*Steel Sparks*, December 4, 1920)

one of the motivations for his emphasis on the success of the Denver store. Both L. R. and Will had adopted sons, and this factor may have enhanced their bond.

Will apparently had connections with the mayor of Denver. A letter from Mayor Bailey welcomed him to the city and encouraged his expansion plans. L. R. loved to have the local politicians involved in his projects because it raised the company's visibility and added instant credibility with the community.

The plan was to build a distinctive four-story building with an ample basement. The top floor was to be a storage area that would hold stock for stores in Greeley, Colorado Springs, and Pueblo that would be built as part of the cluster concept. The cafeteria would be in the basement, and the other three floors would be for merchandise. Steel's Department Store would be a destination for shopping, entertainment, and socializing, and it would be on the busiest corner in town. They wanted the following to become the swell local slogan: "Meet Me at Steel's Corner." Well-known Denver architect M. A. Hoyt submitted a drawing, and L. R. loved it.

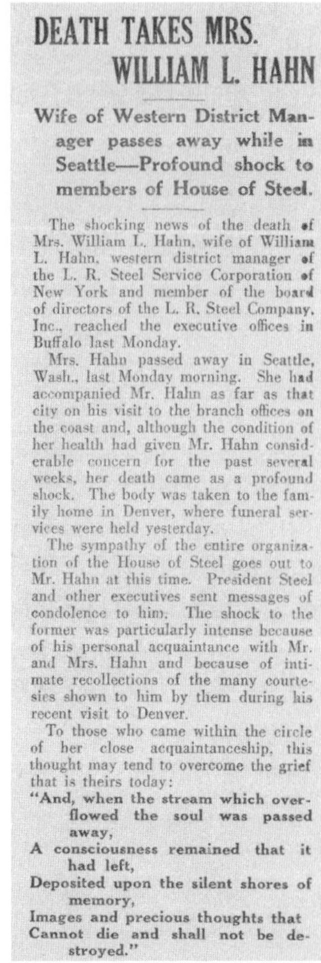

DEATH TAKES MRS. WILLIAM L. HAHN

Wife of Western District Manager passes away while in Seattle—Profound shock to members of House of Steel.

The shocking news of the death of Mrs. William L. Hahn, wife of William L. Hahn, western district manager of the L. R. Steel Service Corporation of New York and member of the board of directors of the L. R. Steel Company, Inc., reached the executive offices in Buffalo last Monday.

Mrs. Hahn passed away in Seattle, Wash., last Monday morning. She had accompanied Mr. Hahn as far as that city on his visit to the branch offices on the coast and, although the condition of her health had given Mr. Hahn considerable concern for the past several weeks, her death came as a profound shock. The body was taken to the family home in Denver, where funeral services were held yesterday.

The sympathy of the entire organization of the House of Steel goes out to Mr. Hahn at this time. President Steel and other executives sent messages of condolence to him. The shock to the former was particularly intense because of his personal acquaintance with Mr. and Mrs. Hahn and because of intimate recollections of the many courtesies shown to him by them during his recent visit to Denver.

To those who came within the circle of her close acquaintanceship, this thought may tend to overcome the grief that is theirs today:

"And, when the stream which overflowed the soul was passed away,
A consciousness remained that it had left,
Deposited upon the silent shores of memory,
Images and precious thoughts that
Cannot die and shall not be destroyed."

93. Death of Will Hahn's wife (*Steel Sparks*, April 2, 1921)

Construction

The first step was to secure a site on the busiest corner in town. The northwest corner of Sixteenth and Welton had been owned by John Good since 1870, and he built an eighteen-room brick home there in 1883. By 1890 the property had become too valuable to be used as a residence, so he tore it down to build a commercial building. This commercial

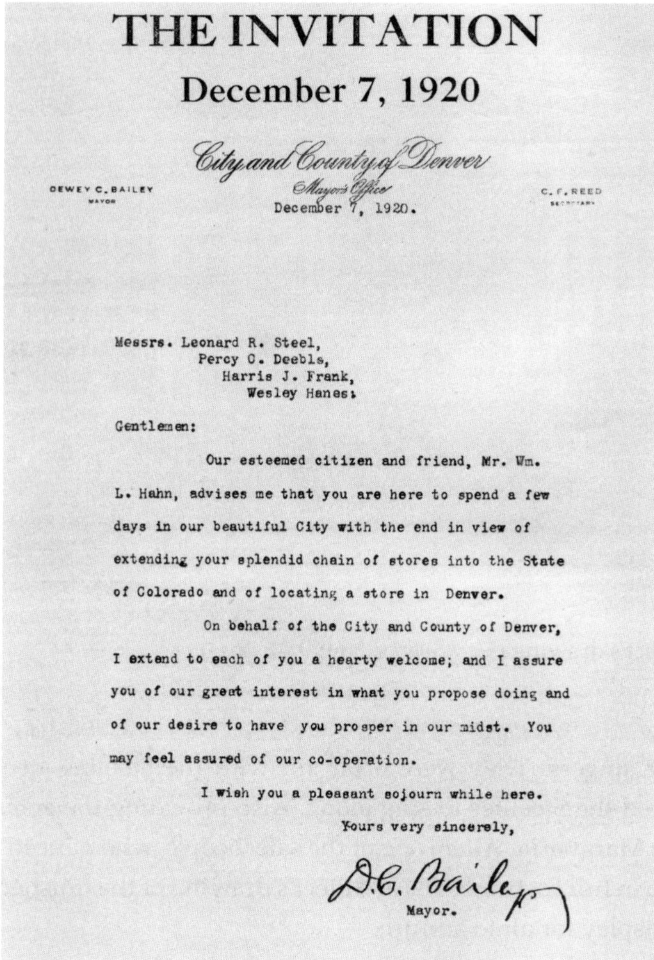

THE INVITATION

December 7, 1920

City and County of Denver

Mayor's Office

DEWEY C. BAILEY
MAYOR

C. F. REED
SECRETARY

December 7, 1920.

Messrs. Leonard R. Steel,
Percy C. Deebls,
Harris J. Frank,
Wesley Hanes:

Gentlemen:

Our esteemed citizen and friend, Mr. Wm. L. Hahn, advises me that you are here to spend a few days in our beautiful City with the end in view of extending your splendid chain of stores into the State of Colorado and of locating a store in Denver.

On behalf of the City and County of Denver, I extend to each of you a hearty welcome; and I assure you of our great interest in what you propose doing and of our desire to have you prosper in our midst. You may feel assured of our co-operation.

I wish you a pleasant sojourn while here.

Yours very sincerely,

D.C. Bailey

Mayor.

94. Letter from Denver's mayor (*Steel Sparks,* December 9, 1922)

building was the one to be replaced by Steel's Department Store. A ninety-nine-year lease was negotiated, and signs immediately appeared on the building announcing the approach of Steel's Department Store. It was never too early to start advertising. The building was demolished on March 1, 1922.

The Denver office celebrated the demolition with . . . what else but a big banquet? Entertainment was provided by the Eurton Orchestra and

AS THE STEEL BUILDING IN DENVER WILL LOOK

Architect's drawing of the building which the L. R. Steel Company, Inc., proposes to erect on the property at the corner of Sixteenth and Welton streets, which has been secured under a ninety-nine year lease.

95. Architect's drawing (*Steel Sparks,* January 8, 1921)

their jazz singers. They were a big hit with the Steelites because they encouraged the Steelites to sing along. Also providing the entertainment was Miss Marguerite Allen, one of the salespeople, who danced a Spanish fandango in full costume. The architect's drawing of the finished building was on display for all to admire.

The entertainment was followed by reading the congratulatory telegrams from other Steel's offices. L. R. sent an inspirational one; others sent poetry or cute sayings. "Congratulations to the men who changed the name of the state to 'Collar-the-Dough,'" wrote C. F. Smythe.

L. R. insisted on being there to turn over the first shovel of dirt. His boyish enthusiasm could not be denied, even if it required a long train trip. He took the train from Buffalo with his wife and a small party of executives and support staff. Included in the party was Harry J. Sprang, official photographer for the corporation. A few more Steelites were picked up when the train stopped in Chicago. All the arrangements for the groundbreaking ceremony were organized by Will Hahn.

96. Sixteenth and Welton Streets before construction (*Steel Sparks,* August 6, 1921)

97. Demolition (*Steel Sparks,* March 11, 1922)

First, though, there needed to be a banquet to celebrate L. R.'s arrival and the pending groundbreaking. A photo of that banquet was taken on Saturday, March 11, 1922. It was not exactly a small banquet, but it was paid for by the House of Steel.

With Will Hahn and a large crowd of well-wishers looking on, L. R. took off his jacket and turned over the first shovel of dirt in the empty lot. Later that evening, he would attend the first public showing of his movie. There were five thousand people in attendance, and hundreds more were turned away.

98. Banquet at the Broadmoor Hotel (*Steel Sparks*, March 18, 1922)

99. The first shovel of dirt (*Steel Sparks*, March 18, 1922)

Five Thousand Crowd Auditorium to See Film Story of Growth of Steel Chain Stores

L. R. Steel, head of all the L. R. Steel organizations, turning the first shovelful of earth for the foundation of the $300,000 store building his corporation will put up at Sixteenth and Welton streets. To the right of Mr. Steel is William L. Hahn, Western representative of the corporation, in charge of the Denver offices. Inserted are pictures of Mr. Steel and Mrs. Steel, who is accompanying him on the tour.

100. The first showing of the film (*Steel Sparks,* March 18, 1922)

It may very well have been the happiest day of his life, perhaps even the happiest moment, and it should have been. Everything worked as planned. All of his big projects were going to be successful. All the years of hard work were being rewarded. All the big ideas were becoming real. Maybe even that far-fetched Niagara Falls idea would work. It was Monday, March 13, 1922, almost exactly one year before his sudden death.

L. R. wrote a message for the March 11, 1922, newsletter before he left for the groundbreaking. He wanted all his employees to read it while the event was happening so that they could all experience his thrill:

> When this reaches the eyes of most of our readers, there will have been enacted in the city of Denver two events that will ever stand out prominently in the records of the progress of our organization. These are the breaking of ground for the construction of our Denver store and the initial public exhibition of "Pennsylvania Hills to the Chain of Steel Industries." Both events assume unusual importance because of the effect they are certain to have on our future.
>
> The building of the Denver store marks a big stride in the expansion of our Steel Store chain, carrying us into new territory that offers a wonderful opportunity. Being built and equipped through the subscriptions of members of our organization, this will be the "Steelites' own store." To those thus interested, it of vital concern because of the benefits that will accrue. To me, this store, as it will be, looms in my vision as a great monument to the loyalty and support of my co-workers.
>
> These are momentous days for the House of Steel, and we are taking full advantage of the opportunities these days offer.

The next week, March 18, 1922, he returned to Buffalo and sent this message to the employees: "The wonderful events that marked my trip to Denver, from which I have just returned, have aroused in me a feeling that is impossible of description in cold type. Aside from my own personal feeling and deep gratification over what transpired, I see in these incidents a great forward step in the steady progress of or enterprises. As for myself, my ambition is to prove in concrete form my sincere appreciation of the great display of loyalty and co-operation that was emphatically given on this occasion as on all others."

Meanwhile, the construction project proceeded. Heavy equipment was brought in for the serious work. In one photo, Will Hahn is holding the shovel that L. R. used. Shovels can last a long time; is that one still around somewhere today?

Special consideration was given to building the foundation. L. R. thought that he might want an eight-story building sometime in the next ten years, so he built a foundation strong enough to support that structure. It was more expensive now, but it would be a good investment when it came time to add on the extra four floors.

STEAM SHOVEL FINISHING WHAT PRESIDENT STEEL STARTED

The big steam shovel is shown taking up the work of excavating for the foundation for the Denver Steel Store after President Steel had turned the first spadeful of ground on Monday, March 13. Inset is seen Western District Manager Will Hahn proudly displaying the spade with which President Steel started the big job.

101. A steam shovel to excavate the foundation (*Steel Sparks*, March 25, 1922)

The Finished Building

Every retailer would love to finish a new building just in time for the Christmas shopping season. L. R. hit his target. Of course, he needed more than just a building in order to open; he shipped twenty-nine boxcars full of merchandise from Chicago to Denver in time to stock the store. Each boxcar had an advertisement on the side saying "Steel's" in big letters. The Denver store was done and ready to open on December 9, 1922.

The four-story building had fifty-three thousand square feet of space. The basement contained the Persian Garden Cafeteria with seating for

102. Work begins (*Steel Sparks,* May 20, 1922; photo taken on March 15, 1922)

103. The foundation being built (*Steel Sparks,* May 20, 1922; photo taken on May 10, 1922)

five hundred people. It was one of the largest eating establishments in the West at that time. There was also a subbasement that probably held the heating system. The first floor had the Mary Lincoln Candy operation and his lingerie, hat, and waist section for women. There was a balcony

"GOING UP!" BUILDING THE STEEL STORE IN DENVER

This picture, taken on June 14, shows the progress that had been made at that time on the construction of the Steel Store in Denver, which will be one of the finest merchandising institutions in the country. With the foundation in place, rapid progress is being made in the erection of the upper floors.

104. Going up (*Steel Sparks,* June 24, 1922; photo taken on June 14, 1922)

RAPID PROGRESS ON THE DENVER STEEL STORE

This picture, made July 12, shows the great strides that are being made in the erection of the Steel Store in Denver, Colo. It will be seen that construction has progressed to the fourth floor and the picture gives an excellent idea of the size of the wonderful merchandising institution that will soon be opened.

105. Rapid progress (*Steel Sparks,* July 22, 1922; photo taken on July 12, 1922)

REVEALING THE BEAUTY OF THE DENVER STEEL STORE

This picture shows how the Steel Store building in Denver, Colo., looked on August 23. From this picture one may gain an excellent idea of the strikingly handsome appearance the building will present when completed.

106. The sign on the second floor says "Meet Me at Steel's Corner" (*Steel Sparks*, September 16, 1922)

107. Finished building (*Steel Sparks*, December 9, 1922)

MERCHANDISE FOR THE DENVER STEEL STORE ENROUTE FROM THE EAST

Some of them look hardly bigger than dots, but if you count them you will find there are twenty-nine cars in this freight train, each loaded with merchandise shipped from New York and other points in the East to Steel's Department Store in Denver for the opening today. The picture was taken after the train had left Chicago for the West.

108. Train with supplies for Denver (*Steel Sparks,* December 9, 1922)

"WORLD'S GREATEST CHAIN STORE" IS OPENED IN DENVER

This picture of the wonderful Steel's Department Store in Denver was made on the afternoon before the opening day, December 9, and gives an idea of the strikingly beautiful appearance of the building, all floors of which were packed with eager shoppers in welcome of this great merchandising institution dedicated to the service of the people.

109. Ready for business in Denver (*Steel Sparks,* December 16, 1922)

over the first floor that contained a beauty shop. The second floor held the totally furnished six-room bungalow that helped shoppers visualize their purchases in a homelike setting. The third floor was a food market, including a fresh fish and meat counter. Presumably, it was on that floor so any odors would be likely to travel up and away without bothering the shoppers. The top floor was for storage so the store could be restocked quickly. There were two elevators for people and one for freight. Throughout the store were electric signs proclaiming, "Nothing Over $20."

L. R. visited Denver again in late October and issued this evaluation in the November 4, 1922, edition of the newsletter:

> Although I had anticipated seeing a very fine building, I was genuinely amazed and pleasantly surprised when, upon my arrival in Denver on Saturday of last week, I gazed upon our store building at Sixteenth and Welton Streets. It is the most magnificent building I have ever seen and it is a fitting monument to all who have assisted in the building or our great companies during the past three years.
>
> The architecture is vastly different and far superior to the ordinary chain store idea. In fact, when completed it will excel the architectural attractiveness of any other great merchandising structures in the United States or Canada.
>
> It is my opinion that this building and this store will constitute a school of merchandising competing with the largest high price department stores for beauty of appearance and results for the next twenty-five years. Every comfort that the rich man finds at the high price stores will be obtainable by the farmer and the poor man in the Denver store, the world's greatest chain store.
>
> The Denver store presents a great inspiration to press forward with our plans to establish Steel stores throughout the continent. Let us all get together and work together to build them everywhere.

The Steelites were encouraged to feel justified pride.

The Grand Opening

As I mentioned in chapter 5, grand openings were big events at Steel's. There was only one problem with the Denver grand opening: L. R. could not attend. On the other hand, it was good news. There were two other grand openings on the same day, December 9, 1922, and even L. R. could not be in Buffalo, Hamilton (Ontario), and Denver all on the same day. He went to Hamilton and left Denver in the able hands of Will Hahn.

110. "Justified Pride" (*Steel Sparks,* December 9, 1922)

L. R. wrote the following message in the December 9, 1922, edition of the newsletter: "In the history of our merchandising business, December 9, 1922, will ever stand out prominently. The significance of the day to us lies in the fact that it is the date of the addition of three great links in our strong and steadily growing international chain of Steel Stores. When this comes under the eye of the reader, our new stores in Denver, Hamilton, and Buffalo will be in operation and humming with business activity."

The Denver grand opening was a mob scene. They locked the doors to help relieve the crush inside, but the police asked Will Hahn to open

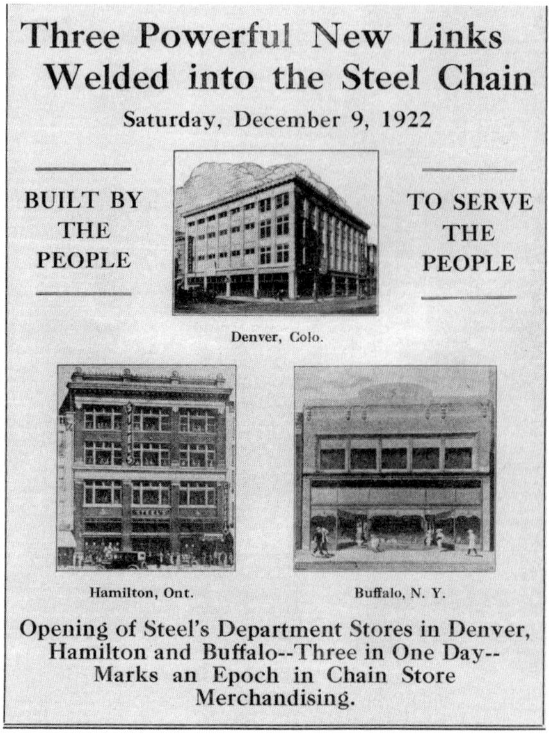

111. Three in one day (*Steel Sparks,* December 9, 1922)

them again because the large crowd outside was blocking traffic. Thousands of people were turned away, while the "conservative" estimate had 125,000 people streaming in and out of the store on Saturday, December 9, 1922. Given that the population of Denver in 1920 was 256,491 (US Census Bureau 1998), that conservative estimate may be a bit off. It is not likely that half the population of the city visited the store on one day, even though Will had arranged for Santa Claus to drive around the city in a truck covered with signs inviting them to "Meet Me at Steel's Corner." The Buffalo opening drew 50,000, while the one in Hamilton had 85,000, give or take a few.

The Persian Garden Cafeteria served 6,000 people on opening day. A six-piece orchestra played while people ate fifty-cent chicken dinners that were "today's special" on the menu. Diners were greeted with a large American eagle carved out of ice flanked by suckling pigs at each end.

112. The fifty-cent chicken special in Denver (*Steel Sparks,* December 23, 1922)

113. The Denver store at night (*Steel Sparks,* January 13, 1923)

On the second day of operation in Denver, Will Hahn sent this telegram to L. R.: "Steel store met with greatest reception at the hands of Denver people imaginable. Bingo! Today is Monday, second day of business. We are overwhelmed with crowds" (*Steel Sparks,* December 16, 1922). That was the top. It could not get any better, and it never did. By the time the beautiful nighttime photo of the Denver store appeared in the January 13, 1923, issue of the newsletter, L. R. was only two weeks away from losing control of his company.

7

The Late-Night Meeting

"Well, Folks, Here We Are"

THE LINCOLN BUILDING in downtown Buffalo was the scene of a heated meeting on Friday, January 26, 1923. Steel's was out of money. They could not pay their bills. A $250,000 payment on a loan that funded the acquisition of the F. E. Nelson stores was due, and they were unable to pay it. It was the final payment of a $1 million loan, so missing the payment would mean that the $750,000 already invested would be wasted when the foreclosure happened.

Other issues must have been discussed, and there were certainly earlier meetings among the concerned senior executives. Some of these people had run other businesses or worked in the chain store industry for years, so their concerns about rapid expansion, big spending, and the carefree use of debt were probably well founded. Still, it must have been difficult for them to plot a coup against their boss, the founder of the company, L. R. Steel.

Somehow, they convinced him to resign. The financial situation must have been obvious, but lack of ready funds had never worried the overly optimistic L. R. They let him retire under the cover of illness and fatigue from overwork. Perhaps he really was too ill to fight against his own managers any longer. He loved his company, so the plotters must have made a convincing case.

L. R. had his supporters. Will Hahn of Denver, his protégé, would certainly have been on his side. Perhaps that explains why he was not included in the new management team, even though the *New York Times* article about the resignation had speculated that he would be the new president (*New York Times* 1923a).

L. R.'s sudden retirement was announced on Saturday, January 27, 1923. But Saturday was the day that the *Steel Sparks* newsletter was released, and it had already been printed. They sent it out with an unintentionally final message from L. R. to his "boys and girls." It was an optimistic view of one of his favorite themes, taking advantage of opportunities.

Following L. R.'s departure, Walter M. Wilkins, general counsel and secretary of the L. R. Steel Company, issued a statement to the press claiming that the financial condition of the company was "extremely satisfactory." He did note, however, that the accounting firm of Marwick, Mitchell & Company would be acting in an advisory capacity on financial matters and would be involved in implementing a budgeting system, something that apparently had been overlooked previously. He also did his best to make it seem like a friendly departure:

> Mr. Steel has crowded the work of a lifetime or more into a space of the last three years and the terrific strain has inevitably told on his physical resources. Over a year ago, his physician advised his retirement from active business or at least a year's complete rest, but, feeling that his work of organization was not then completed, he has persevered in his work at great danger to his health.
>
> Mr. Steel leaves the companies with the admiration and highest personal regard of those who have worked with him and who appreciate his creative genius and have wondered at his dynamic force. No one without

WE have been told that the year we are now in is one of greatest opportunity. There is every reason for confidence that this is so, but it cannot be any more a time of opportunity than the past has been unless we make it so. Real opportunity is not born of conditions that exist, but of conditions as we make them. Opportunity belongs to no one time or place, but is as universal as the air. Success resolves itself down to the question of recognizing opportunity.

With the dawn of every day comes new opportunities. An eminent business man once said, "It is time that establishes an equal opportunity for all." It is, therefore, up to each one of us to recognize and take advantage of our opportunities if we would gain the objective we have in view, for what you are is the answer to how you have spent your time.

When you read this, just pause a moment and see if there is not right before you an opportunity, which, if you will take advantage of it, will find you at the end of the day in a better position than you were before. The work you are engaged in is one of perpetual opportunity.

There is plenty of room on the ladder of success for those who will devote the necessary energy to climbing and, when the start is made, each succeeding step will be easier to accomplish.

L. R. STEEL, President.

114. L. R.'s last message (*Steel Sparks,* January 27, 1923)

> such qualities and the quality of inspiring leadership could accomplish what he has done in the past three years. (*Steel Sparks*, February 3, 1923)

L. R. turned over a large quantity of stock that represented his controlling interest in the various companies. No severance package was mentioned. He went back to Marguerite Manor to sulk and refused to talk to the reporters who called.

The New Management

Control of the company passed to a board of managers composed of current Steel's executives who understood the business. The following is an introduction of the men who were successful at removing L. R. from his company:

> Walter M. Wilkins, chairman of the Board of Managers, has been associated with the Steel Enterprises since a short time after the inception of the organization. In his position as general counsel and secretary of the various companies, he has been a most important factor in the development and progress of the business of the companies. His strong personality, trained mind and oft demonstrated ability have been a valuable asset in the past and these qualities, together with the knowledge and experience gained through his association with the steel Enterprises mark him as supremely qualified for the chairmanship of the board that will guide the future activities of the companies.

115. Walter M. Wilkins (*Steel Sparks*, February 3, 1923)

> Mr. Wilkins has been a resident of Buffalo all his life, and is held in high esteem in the legal profession of that city. He was graduated from Princeton University in 1910, and from Harvard Law School in 1913. In September, 1913, he became associated with Kenefick, Cooke, Mitchell and Bass, in the general practice of law.
>
> During his seven years' association with that firm, one of the most widely known in

the country, having the largest professional and legal staff of any firm in New York State, outside of New York City, Mr. Wilkins had extensive experience in general corporate and tax matters and also as an officer and director in numerous corporations, including manufacturing, investment securities, merchandising, etc.

Paul L. Chase, who becomes President of the L. R. Steel Service Corporation of New York, assumes that office with a firm foundation based on experience gained not only in the Steel Service but in other enterprises. He is one of the oldest members, in point of service, of the Service Corporation, and no little amount of the growth and success of that branch of the organization is attributable to his untiring efforts and ability. Mr. Chase became associate with the Service Corporation as superintendent of offices when it was in its infancy, and has been an important factor in the development of the Service to its present status. His selection to be President of the corporation is a logical step.

116. Paul L. Chase (*Steel Sparks,* February 3, 1923)

Everett C. George, President of the L. R. Steel Company, Inc., has been associated with the organization for the last two years and during the last six months has been general manager of Steel Stores in the United States. Mr. George is thoroughly a "chain store" man, having spent practically all of his mature years in that business. For 20 years he was connected with the Woolworth Chain Store System and other leading chain store concerns. His status in the merchandising world is high and under his guidance the business of the steel Chain Stores is in most capable hands.

117. Everett C. George (*Steel Sparks,* February 3, 1923)

Frank J. Rohr, President of the Steel Realty Development Corporation, is another veteran member of the Steel organization, his

118. Frank J. Rohr (*Steel Sparks,* February 3, 1923)

association dating from the early days of the companies. Upon the organization of the Steel Realty Development Corporation, Mr. Rohr, in the capacity of Vice-President and General Manager, took immediate charge of its affairs and directed the work that brought about the efficient organization that exists today. Mr. Rohr is one of the prominent younger business men of Buffalo, whose experience in the business world in general and with the Steel Realty Development Corporation in particular, eminently qualifies him for the position as head of the Realty Branch of the Steel Enterprises and as a member of the governing board.

119. W. A. Holzworth (*Steel Sparks,* February 3, 1923)

William A. Holzworth, Vice-president of the L. R. Steel Company, Inc., has been in the chain store business since his youth, having "grown up" in the business. He is experienced in all branches and phases of chain store merchandising, having begun his career at the bottom of the ladder, filling minor position and working his way steadily upward. He has been associated with various chain store companies and was one of the executives of the Holzworth Stores when that chain was acquired by the L. R. Steel Company, at which time he became associated with the latter. Mr. Holzworth's knowledge and ability have been of great value in the development of the Steel Stores in the past, and, in his new and greater capacity will prove of even greater value in the future.

Paul Chase, the leader of the sales force, took over L. R.'s column in the newsletter. In his first message, he said, "Well, folks, here we are. We have a big job on our hands, but this is nothing new for us." (*Steel Sparks,* February 3, 1923)

The Quick Fall

The new management had no magic. They defaulted on the $250,000 loan for the Nelson chain after trying to get a loan from other sources to cover it. Word spread quickly, as the *New York Times* and other newspapers covered the story. Other creditors, such as National Toy and Tinsel Manufacturing Company of Manitowoc, Wisconsin, sued over unpaid bills. Everybody wanted to be paid, and there was no money to do so.

In addition to loans, Steel's had two main sources of revenue. The income from the stores, more than $9 million in 1922, was really a net loss. With high overhead and very low prices, the stores were never profitable. No amount of volume could make up for that fact. Revenue had been rising rapidly. It increased about 20 percent in 1922 after growing almost 200 percent in 1921, but revenue is not profit.

The other source of revenue was the sale of stock in the various companies. This operation was very profitable, but it was stopped cold on February 20, 1923, when the Maryland attorney general issued an order restraining the sale of stock (*New York Times* 1923d). Although his order was effective only in Maryland, publicity from it made sales in other states difficult. The New York attorney general stopped all stock sales on March 1, 1923 (*New York Times* 1923c).

The legal basis for the restraining order was a potential violation of the "blue-sky laws." Steel's was not charged with a violation, but they were forbidden from selling any more stock until the investigation was finished. Blue-sky laws are state laws intended to protect the public from the sale of fraudulent securities, that is, securities that are "backed by nothing but the blue skies of Kansas." The first blue-sky law was passed in Kansas in 1911, and many other states, including New York, soon followed. There were no federal regulations about stock sales until the Securities and Exchange Commission (SEC) was founded in 1934, so this uneven web of various state laws provided the only legal framework.

L. R. was well aware of these regulations on the sale of securities. In May 1921, he hired an attorney specifically to help the company stay in compliance. George C. Speer had fathered the Kentucky blue-sky laws when he was a state senator, so he had an ideal background for his role with Steel's (*Steel Sparks*, May 28, 1921).

Good intentions had no effect. The state investigation removed Steel's only realistic source of income. Salespeople, with nothing to sell, drifted away. The stores remained open and the cafeterias still served chicken dinners, but more loans went into default and more vendors went unpaid.

The New York State investigation showed that Steel's was getting ready to sell $30 million in stock. They had already sold $26 million to about sixty thousand people, so they planned to pay the bills by more of the same. It might have worked, at least for a while, but they were not allowed to do it.

L. R. had been a hero on the way up, but he was now castigated by the press and the shareholders. There were complaints about the big incomes made by Steelites. Some salespeople made as much as $2,000 per week (adjusted for inflation, that amount would be about $26,000 per week in current dollars) (US Department of Labor 2011), and L. R.'s stenographer was paid an extravagant $125 per week ($1,600 in current dollars). People wanted to know what happened to their money. Because it disappeared, there must have been a crime. The press coverage turned nasty.

In retrospect, there were warning signs. The big 1922 convention was canceled in favor of a series of smaller regional conventions. Also, on August 22, 1922, L. R. announced the acquisition of the twenty-six drug stores in the Miller-Strong chain, but this topic was never discussed again. It must be assumed that the deal fell through, probably due to financing problems.

Bankruptcy

On March 9, 1923, President Harding was just starting his vacation in Indian River, Florida. A crowd of twenty-five thousand people had just seen Harry F. Young, the "Human Fly," fall to his death while climbing the Hotel Martinique in New York City as part of a stunt to promote a Harold Lloyd film. And L. R. Steel's business empire declared bankruptcy.

At that time, it consisted of twenty corporations operating in eighteen states with an alleged value of twenty million dollars. Receivers were appointed by the court to keep the businesses in operation while an audit was started to reveal the true financial condition. The goal was to prevent a sudden collapse, pay the creditors, and preserve some value for the shareholders.

The investors demanded their money back, but it was too late. The perpetual-motion machine stalled and was not likely to start up again. Angry crowds poured into the Lincoln Building in downtown Buffalo, and a deputy attorney general came in from Albany to hear their complaints. A group of disgruntled shareholders formed a committee to demand justice and seek the return of their money.

The audit that was the first step in the bankruptcy did not go well. Auditors from Marwick, Mitchell & Company missed several predicted delivery dates because the internal accounting was more complex than they anticipated. First, there were twenty different companies, and it seems that their finances had not always been clearly separated. And then there were complications in valuing the stock that had been sold. It

120. Marguerite Manor while L. R. is in seclusion (*Buffalo Courier Express*, March 11, 1923)

was a big problem to figure out how much stock was sold on the partial payment plan. A down payment of eighty dollars could buy two hundred dollars' worth of stock, but it seems that the records were not kept in a consistent fashion. Of course, there was no chance of collecting the remaining amount.

The receivers took a train to Denver to personally inspect the best store in the chain. It had no debt, courtesy of the Steelites who donated the money to build it.

On May 28, 1923, the auditors made a preliminary report that sixty thousand investors had invested more than twenty million dollars, three times the size of Charles Ponzi's better-known scheme from the prior year. This estimate included just the US operations, not Canadian. Other estimates had the total at twenty-six million dollars, if Canada was included. They thought three million dollars might be left, but it was too early to be certain.

Employees were laid off, others took pay cuts, some stores were closed, and the sales force was gone. Only twenty-three stores were left. People still shopped at the remaining Steel's stores and ate chicken dinners at the cafeterias, but there were no more grand openings with brass bands.

L. R.'s empire crumbled while he stayed in seclusion at Marguerite Manor with his wife. He accepted no visitors. He was plotting.

8

L. R.'s Last Train Ride

"I Was Awakened by a Peculiar Sound"

The Train to Chicago

L. R. grew restless at Marguerite Manor. Both federal and state authorities were auditing his records for evidence of fraud, illegal use of the mails, or any other irregularities. Also, winters in Buffalo are not likely to lift the spirits of someone who has just lost his empire and is in the process of losing his reputation. He was used to action, to being the one with the big idea and the devoted employees working to make it happen. He did not feel well, but was not good at convalescing.

He put together a plan to buy back controlling interest in his shrinking, bankrupt empire. He did not wait for the audit to be finished and provide the actual worth of the remaining companies; he settled on one million dollars as the amount he needed, and he decided to borrow it. It was a time when anything was possible, so it might have worked. He lined up meetings with bankers in Pittsburgh, Cleveland, and Chicago. If the rumors were right, he also scheduled a meeting with one of the richest men in America, Henry Ford. The plan was to see all of them on one train trip and then continue west to someplace warm, possibly Arizona, where he could use the one million dollars he had just borrowed to negotiate the repurchase of his empire while improving his health in the sun.

In the old days, he traveled with a large, happy group of executives eager to win his favor. On this trip, he had only two companions, his British chauffeur, Ernest Matty, and J. O. Dozois, a loyal former employee who had worked as a buyer. As usual, they traveled in style, staying in a Pullman sleeping car. They first went to Pittsburgh, and then to Cleveland. The meetings did not go well. Both bankers turned down his big idea.

Before boarding the night train from Cleveland to Chicago, L. R. called his wife at Marguerite Manor to tell her of his rejections and to

121. Marguerite Steel (*Buffalo Times*, March 23, 1923)

discuss the health-giving value of the warm weather that he was going to see when he got to the Southwest. The next call she received, four hours later, was from J. O. Dozois, informing her of L. R.'s death.

The End

As they walked through the Cleveland train station, L. R.'s companions noticed that he was limping. His left foot kept turning in awkwardly, and he seemed to be having trouble controlling it. They boarded New York Central No. 89, westbound for Chicago, on the evening of March 21, 1923. His chauffeur described what happened as the train was pulling into Union Station at Toledo, Ohio:

> Mr. Steel, Mr. J. O. Dozois of Cleveland and I retired about 11 P.M. Mr. Dozois had a berth in another car while I slept in a berth above that occupied by Mr. Steel. At 1:10 A.M. I was awakened by a peculiar sound made by Mr. Steel. I had never heard him make that kind of a noise before so I leaned over and asked him what was the matter.
>
> He was lying on his back. His hands and feet were twitching in a convulsive manner. A little bit of froth was oozing from his mouth. I climbed down and lifted him up, calling him by name. I thought at first he was merely having a nightmare. He did not speak. I put a pillow under his head and rang for the porter to call Mr. Dozois. I asked the

122. Toledo's Union Station in 1925 (courtesy of the Toledo-Lucas County Public Library, http://images2.toledolibrary.org/)

> conductor to get a doctor and he said we would be in the union station in five minutes and we could get one then. The conductor felt Mr. Steel's pulse and said it was very faint. As I held him in my arms he suddenly became limp. I did not know he was dead until we reached the station. (*Toledo Blade* 1923)

L. R. lived exactly forty-four years, eleven months, and five days.

The Aftermath

The sudden death of a famous person who happened to be traveling through Toledo made the front page of the local papers.

At about two in the morning, the body, still wearing pajamas, was taken from the train to H. H. Birkenkamp Undertaking. The coroner was called to investigate. News spread quickly, and more than two hundred people gathered at the funeral home for a look. It was not mentioned how many of them were disgruntled investors, but Steel's did have an office in Toledo that closed in February. That office had sold about $100,000 worth of stock to four hundred people during the two years that it was open.

Rumors soon started. Was he poisoned? Did an angry investor get to his food? There was also a rumor that he was carrying $19,000 with him,

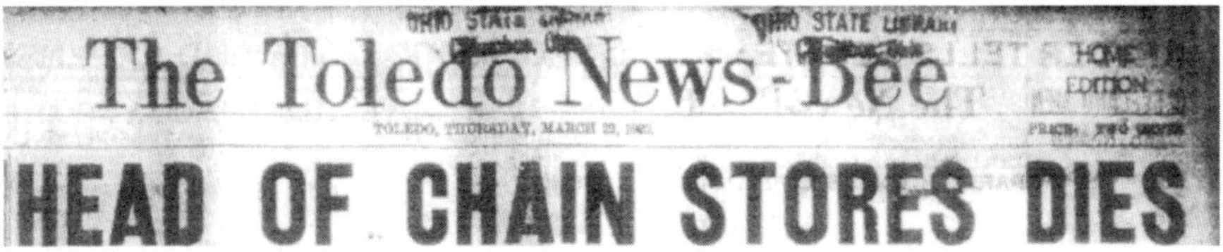

The Toledo News-Bee

HOME EDITION

HEAD OF CHAIN STORES DIES

123. Front-page news (*Toledo News-Bee*, March 22, 1923)

but it vanished after he died. These rumors were proven to be false. The coroner found $476 in his clothes; if someone was going to steal money from a dead man's body, they probably would have taken it all.

The autopsy found no evidence of poison. They did find a broken blood vessel in L. R.'s brain. The cause of death was listed as apoplexy, a term that is no longer used. Today, it would be called a stroke. They also found an abnormal heart ("extremely fatty"), liver problems, and evidence of high blood pressure. The coroner noted that stress from exertion and rejection, combined with an autocratic disposition, probably helped cause the apoplexy.

Later on, his supporters claimed that he died of a broken heart. This notion may not be as far-fetched as it might seem at first. Recent medical research supports the view that stressful events and personality type can be risk factors for strokes (House et al. 1990).

The Funeral

Immediately after the autopsy, L. R.'s body was put back on a train headed for Buffalo, with Ernest Matty attending. A small group of friends and former employees greeted the train as it arrived. Walter M. Wilkins and Frank Rohr were among them. The men removed their hats to show respect as the casket passed into the waiting hearse. His wife stayed at Marguerite Manor with their son because she was too upset to leave.

The body was taken to a local funeral home and then to Marguerite Manor for the funeral. A mahogany coffin lined with copper and silver was selected.

The brief but impressive service at Marguerite Manor was performed by Rev. Walter R. Lord of Saint John's Episcopal Church. The service drew a crowd of 350 people, including friends, former employees, and relatives, but it did not include his wife. She was too upset to leave her room. She knew that she would not be able to control herself when they played L. R.'s favorite song, "Beautiful Isle of Somewhere." (This song can be heard at http://nethymnal.org/htm/b/e/beautisl.htm.)

The audit was halted on the afternoon of the funeral so the office staff could attend. All of Steel's remaining businesses paused for ten minutes during the funeral. Puzzled patrons at the Buffalo cafeteria looked up from their chicken dinners as the staff stopped service to cry and sing "Auld Lang Syne."

A long line of cars left Getzville and proceeded down Main Street to Forest Lawn Cemetery. The local papers reported that a chilly March wind blew through the canvas tent erected over the grave site as the coffin was lowered. Marguerite was able to attend, but wept uncontrollably. The papers said she sobbed, "Leonard, oh Leonard . . . My God, oh My God," as Carl Cochems, who had helped create the movie, tried to comfort her. Philip, their fourteen-year-old son, seemed dazed and stood as closely as possible to his mother with a pained and frightened look.

124. Walter M. Wilkins leads the pallbearers (*Buffalo Courier Express*, March 25, 1923)

125. The funeral procession (*Buffalo Courier Express,* March 25, 1923)

126. Philip Steel (*Buffalo Courier Express,* March 25, 1923)

The newspapers that had been critical of him in life were gentle at his death. "Relatives, friends and business associates looked for the last time at the man who, they believed, meant well, but fell short of his aim" (*Buffalo Courier Express* 1923). A company official made this comment to the reporters at the funeral: "No matter what the opinion of the public at large

127. L. R.'s grave in Forest Park (photo by Dave Dyer)

may be, you surely can see how beloved the man was by his close associates and subordinates. Had fate not turned her back on him, he would be alive today and looked upon with reverence by everyone. His brain child broke down and he, its father, broke his heart over it" (*Buffalo Times* 1923).

A small, inexpensive marker can still be found in Forest Park. It seems too simple a monument for a man with such great aspirations. On the other hand, it was probably ordered after they found out that he died broke. There was not even enough money to pay his funeral expenses.

His Will

L. R. signed his will on January 6, 1923. This must have been a difficult time for him; he was ill, and he was in the process of losing control of his empire. Still, he had time to be generous to others. Walter Wilkins, who would be the new president of the company within weeks, was the executor.

Generous monetary bequests were made to Marguerite and son Philip. They also were to get the home, his pool table, and all the equipment in the bowling alley at Marguerite Manor. Money was left for three churches near his hometown in Pennsylvania.

He set aside ten thousand dollars to create a trust fund to cover the cost of placing flowers and wreaths on his grave and on the graves of various relatives and friends every year on his three favorite holidays, Decoration Day, Mother's Day, and Christmas.

It did not make any difference. The will was probated in April 1923, and it was soon revealed that he owned no assets that could be turned into cash. All his savings were in the stock in his own company, and it was now worthless. No money was available to make his promises come true. He might as well have left Niagara Falls to his heirs.

In December 1922, he sold his Lafayette Avenue home for twenty thousand dollars, netting thirteen thousand dollars after the balance due on the mortgage. That money was used to pay his income tax bill, so it was gone.

L. R. had a life insurance policy worth one hundred thousand dollars, but it ended up providing no funds for his heirs. The policy was originally taken out with Niagara Life Insurance Company, but they had been taken over by Metropolitan Life. L. R. needed to sign and return a document approving the transfer of his policy to Metropolitan, but, for some unknown reason, it never happened. Metropolitan used this technicality to deny payment. It would not have made any difference if he had signed it; his company, not his family, was listed as the beneficiary.

His estate owed sixty thousand dollars for income taxes, and the remaining physical assets, such as Marguerite Manor, were sold to pay down part of this debt. Of course, the acreage that had been turned into a chicken farm had previously been sold to his company, so he owned only the home, garage, and front lawn. Marguerite told the press that she had no plans, and it was true.

9

Was It a Ponzi Scheme?

Would a Crook Live Next to a Chicken Farm?

L. R. and Ponzi

Leonard Rambler Steel and Charles Ponzi had a lot in common. They were both snappy dressers who had many loyal followers. They were both known for their personal generosity and donations to charity. They were both extremely devoted to their mothers. They were both optimists who had great faith in themselves. Ponzi was so confident that he had no savings at all, and L. R. had all his savings in the stock his company sold. Both were happily married with devoted wives, but neither had biological children (L. R.'s son was adopted). Both were likable, driven leaders, and both died of strokes. Also, both put together schemes that relied on getting small sums of money from a large number of people.

L. R.'s stock scandal was actually larger than Ponzi's, although it was not nearly as well known. Ponzi had twenty thousand investors who invested a total of about $8 million (about $400 each) (Zuckoff 2005, 298). L. R.'s sixty thousand investors contributed approximately $26 million (about $433 each). L. R.'s stock sale would be about $350 million in 2011 dollars adjusted for inflation (US Department of Labor 2011).

Remarkably, they started their businesses within thirty days of each other in 1919. Ponzi's scheme lasted only until the end of the summer in 1920 because it attracted the attention of the authorities immediately. He promised outrageous returns of 50 percent in only forty-five days from investing in something that most people did not understand, International Reply Coupons. An IRC is a government document that can be exchanged for postage stamps.

The following describes how Ponzi's IRC scheme was supposed to work. If you send a letter to someone in a foreign country and want to include the postage for them to reply, you can do it with an International Reply Coupon.

If I send a letter to someone in Italy, it would be difficult for me to include the Italian stamp needed for a reply, as they are not normally sold here. It would also be difficult for me to include cash or a check, because the US dollar is not the currency used in Italy. A self-addressed, stamped envelope would be worthless, because a foreign stamp would not work in Italy.

To resolve this problem, most of the world's post offices agreed to accept IRCs. The sender buys an IRC at his local post office for the cost of first-class postage on a letter. The IRC is included in the letter and can be redeemed in the recipient's country for a first-class postage stamp. The IRC became, essentially, an international currency that was accepted at post offices around the world.

Ponzi, who was a stamp collector, saw an opportunity. The cost of postage varied from country to country. If he bought $1.00 worth of coupons in Italy, he could trade them for $3.30 worth of postage stamps in Boston (Zuckoff 2005, 95). He could, potentially, make $2.30 from each dollar invested, a 230 percent profit. We should not be surprised to see why he felt comfortable paying 50 percent interest on money he borrowed.

Most investors will recognize this technique as an arbitrage strategy: buy a commodity where it is cheap, and sell it quickly in a market where it will bring more. There is nothing illegal about doing it. If markets are very inefficient, it can be a successful strategy.

However, Ponzi quickly found that it was easier to get people to invest in the scheme than to actually run the business of buying IRCs in Italy and selling them in America. If he had really tried to do it, he would have found that there is no ready market for IRCs, at least at full price, because stamps are readily available. Also, he would have encountered transportation costs and the fact that IRCs were used only infrequently. His false claims about the underlying business were a crime when they were used to induce investments.

As more money started flowing into the scheme, Ponzi used money from new investors to pay the old investors. Obviously, this arrangement could not last very long, and it didn't. When the scheme got in trouble, one of his plans was to start a new company, possibly a bank, and use the profits from this company to make his original company solvent. This idea did not work, either.

Ponzi and L. R. were contemporaries, but there is no evidence that they ever met or had any influence on each other. The glaring difference between L. R.'s business and Ponzi's is that L. R. really did have an underlying business. There were at least seventy-five stores in operation, and there was an honest effort to make them successful. It turned out that it was much easier to make money by selling stock in the businesses than by running the businesses, but at least there was a business. L. R. fell to the temptation of easy money, as many people have. L. R. was not running a scheme that was clearly fraudulent like Ponzi's. He promised only a 7 percent annual return, not 50 percent in forty-five days. He was not lying about the underlying business.

On the other hand, it does seem that L. R.'s enterprise of twenty companies had one important characteristic of a Ponzi scheme, that is, existing investors were paid with funds from new investors. It sounds dangerously close to a Rob-Peter-to-Pay-Paul scheme. Money from stock sales was not kept strictly with the company that was represented by the stock.

This lack of accounting discipline seems to have been practiced regularly and openly, with no indication that it might be improper. This quote from L. R. during a speech at the dedication of the new Montreal store provides a clear view of his thinking: "We have done more in one year than any other store system in the world. The Stores Company controls the Service Company. When we get through with the Weeghman Issue, the cost of the stores promotion will have been wiped out. We have sold ten million dollars' worth of securities during the past year. That is only a drop in the bucket to what we are going to do in 1921" (*Steel Sparks*, January 22, 1921). If there was any intent to defraud, he would not have been so open about it. In fact, L. R. wanted to organize his stores so that he had a separate corporation in each state and a separate stock issue for each corporation. It may look suspicious to start twenty companies in succession, sell stock in all them, and use the proceeds from the most recent ones to pay the earlier investors, but at least L. R.'s intent was probably innocent.

There are other real differences between L. R. and Ponzi. Ponzi was a criminal who had served hard time for bank fraud and went on to participate in other dishonest business deals (selling swamp land in Florida). His intent was always to defraud.

The press tried to find prior legal problems for L. R., but all they could come up with was a 1917 case in which he was accused of spreading false rumors about a competitor so that he could buy it at a better price (*Buffalo Express* 1923). This situation happened when he was head of the Metropolitan stores. They said there was an indictment, but it was later thrown out. This case hardly counts as a criminal history, especially when compared to Ponzi's past.

The *Boston Post* won a Pulitzer Prize in 1921 for its series of articles that helped bring down Ponzi. Another Boston newspaper may have tried to do the same thing to L. R. While giving a speech in Boston during the summer of 1921, L. R. referred to an article in a Boston newspaper that was critical of him (*Steel Sparks,* June 25, 1921). The newspaper was not the *Boston Post.* I searched the April, May, and June 1921 editions of the *Boston Post* and found no articles on Steel. This public criticism seems to have been an isolated incident, and L. R.'s ultimate failure was the failure of the underlying business and not the result of his stock sales.

Until his dying day, L. R. was trying to raise money for his business. His business, not his family, was the beneficiary of his life insurance policy. And he lived next to a chicken farm so that he would have a reliable supply of chickens for his cafeterias. Would a crook have done that?

Both men sold dreams, but at least L. R.'s had some possibility of coming true. Ponzi had an idea; L. R. had a business. L. R. sold dreams, too, but there was a real business with real stores, real candy, and real chickens.

The Indictments

A large amount of money went into Steel's stock, and it seemed to have vanished. Angry shareholders encouraged federal and state officials to look for criminal behavior. It would have been politically difficult for officials to ignore sixty thousand unhappy people who thought they had been robbed.

L. R. did not live long enough to face the humiliation of being formally charged with a crime; he died three months before the indictments were announced. Perhaps he would have handled it with more grace than Ponzi did. It is hard to imagine L. R. waving a loaded pistol at a group of reporters.

There were two simultaneous investigations. The federal investigation looked for evidence of mail fraud, one of the charges brought against Ponzi. This investigation was not successful in producing any charges.

On the other hand, the State of New York grand jury returned indictments against some former officers of Steel's. The illustrations show the relevant sections of the New York Penal Code.

After a week of presentations at the Buffalo courthouse by Guy B. Moore, the district attorney, six former officials of the L. R. Steel Company were indicted. Walter M. Wilkins, former general counsel for the company and president at the time of bankruptcy, was the most prominent person indicted. He was charged with a violation of subsection 7 that involved the improper receipt of commissions from the sale of stock. Paul L. Chase, head of the sales organization, was charged with four counts of grand larceny in connection with stock sales. Arthur J. Todd, who was in charge of the branch sales offices, was charged with three counts of grand larceny. James R. Nicholson, treasurer and director, was charged with improper receipt of commissions, just as Wilkins was. Francis J. Rohr, president of the real estate development company, was also indicted for improper receipt of commissions. The name of the sixth indicted official was not released, but it was announced that Gerald K. Rudulph, the original editor of the *Steel Sparks* newsletter who went on to be in charge of advertising, was investigated but not charged.

All of the indicted officials pleaded not guilty and were released on bail. No trials were ever scheduled, and all the charges were eventually dropped, giving support to the view that the charges were mainly a political statement.

The Erie County Clerk's Office could not locate court records from this case, but I was able to find the documentation relating to the dismissal of charges against Walter M. Wilkins. He first petitioned the court for the right to examine the minutes from the grand jury, and this petition was granted in 1925. After reviewing the minutes, he asked the court to dismiss his indictment on the basis that his compensation was for legal

INDICT 6 OFFICIALS IN L. R. STEEL CRASH

Grand Jury Charges Violation of Corporation Laws and Larceny in Stock Sales.

128. The indictments (*New York Times*, June 23, 1923)

§ **664. Misconduct of officers and directors of stock corporations.**

A director of a stock corporation, who concurs in any vote or act of the directors of such corporation, or any of them, by which it is intended:

1. To make a dividend, except from the surplus profits arising from the business of the corporation, and in the cases and manner allowed by law; or,

129. *Penal Law and the Code of Criminal Procedure of the State of New York* (Albany: Matthew Bender, 1911), 131. Digitized from Harvard Law Library by Google Books.

7. Sells, or agrees to sell, or is directly or indirectly interested in the sale of any share of stock of such corporation, or in any agreement to sell the same, unless at the time of such sale or agreement he is an actual owner of such share,

Is guilty of a misdemeanor, punishable by imprisonment for not less than six months, or by a fine not exceeding five thousand dollars, or by both.

130. *Penal Law and the Code of Criminal Procedure of the State of New York* (Albany: Matthew Bender, 1911), 131. Digitized from Harvard Law Library by Google Books.

131. Arthur J. Todd (*Steel Sparks,* December 24, 1920)

132. Gerald K. Rudulph (*Steel Sparks,* July 24, 1920)

work and that he was not compensated for the sale of stock. In addition, he argued that he was not paid with money from the sale of stock; the money was actually generated from the sale of subscriptions to buy stock: "that the commissions were derived by the L. R. Steel Service Corporation upon the taking of stock subscriptions only; and that none of them were commissions upon the sale of any issued and outstanding stock" (Erie County Supreme Court 1926).

The legal point is that subsection 7 is violated only by receiving commissions from stock sales in the secondary market. Once stock is trading openly, corporate officials should not be involved with any transactions in a way that might influence the price. Corporate officials were forbidden from receiving commissions for brokering stock transactions in the open market, although they were allowed to sell stock that they personally owned. However, subsection 7 does not apply to stock sold directly by the company in a primary offering. Steel's stock was sold directly to the public in a subscription agreement that allowed the purchaser to buy the stock on an installment plan, so it would have been a primary offering and it would have been appropriate for company officials to be paid for organizing these transactions. The indictments for the other Steelites were probably dismissed on similar grounds.

Perhaps it was just a coincidence, but Walter M. Wilkins immediately took a job as assistant district attorney for Erie County, working for district attorney Guy B. Moore, the same government official who had recently indicted him.

10

What Went Wrong?

Failure Is an Option

The Structure of Failure

The newspapers reported the story as if crimes were committed, but, in the end, it was a story about the failure of a very creative and aggressive business that lost money. There is nothing illegal about losing money.

Business failures tend to follow a predictable pattern. Jim Collins, in *How the Mighty Fall and Why Some Companies Never Give In* (2009), has researched business failures to reveal the following common stages:

1. hubris due to prior success
2. undisciplined pursuit of more
3. denial of risk and peril
4. grasping for salvation
5. capitulation to irrelevance or death

These are stages, not necessarily causes, of decline. With that idea in mind, it is instructive to see how closely Steel's followed this model.

Stage 1: Hubris Due to Prior Success

L. R.'s Big Idea started out by providing a lot of cheap capital to fund growth. It allowed him to open new stores with brass bands and expensive promotions. The common claim was that Steel's would be the greatest chain store in the world, and his early success made it look like a real possibility. Excessive pride can be seen in the giant October 1921 convention in Buffalo. Nothing was too good for the Steelites, because they were special people. Pride also showed up in the flashy clothes, expensive offices filled with flowers, and big banquets to celebrate every occasion.

Stage 2: Undisciplined Pursuit of More

The income from the stock sales made it possible for Steel's to grow without waiting for the stores to become profitable. More stores, even if not profitable, made it possible to sell more stock. The discipline to run a profitable business was never developed because it was not required. Instead, the goal was more stores, more employees, more salespeople, more companies, and more stock offerings to sell.

Stage 3: Denial of Risk and Peril

L. R. saw no risk in expanding into new businesses, like the coal mine and the sugar plantation, where he had no expertise. He saw no risk in taking on large amounts of debt to buy other stores. Competitors were no risk because they could always be bought. The Niagara Falls International Exposition was to be the largest project of all, but his approach was to start off with an expensive party for fifteen hundred people that might have been more appropriate for the project's completion.

Stage 4: Grasping for Salvation

When they were unable to make the $250,000 payment on the acquisition of the Nelson stores, the first option was to take on more debt. The auditors found that they were planning to issue $30 million worth of stock. During his last train ride, L. R. was desperately trying to save the company by taking on one more big loan.

Stage 5: Capitulation to Irrelevance or Death

L. R.'s death and the bankruptcy of the company were the final stage of decline.

Extravagance

Too many free lollipops for the kids, too many banquets for the Steelites, too many free chicken dinners for the soldiers, too many food baskets for the poor at Christmas, too many superdeals at unbelievable prices—it was too much of everything.

133. Too many baskets of free food for the poor at Christmas (*Steel Sparks,* December 31, 1920)

The international exposition at Niagara Falls was a prime example of L. R.'s extravagance. He spent $180,000 on plans, and parties to celebrate the plans, for an asset that he did not own and had no possibility of acquiring. Even in the age where anything was possible, there were consequences for being wrong.

L. R. wanted more of everything except profits. Financial results are always discussed in terms of sales, sales growth, and the amount of stock sold. Profits were not mentioned. Dividends, usually 7 percent annually, were paid from "surplus," not profits.

Other Problems

Part of L. R.'s problem was that he was operating in a world with few rules. The Securities and Exchange Commission was still ten years away, and the boundless enthusiasm of entrepreneurs like L. R. was limited only by the persuasiveness of their salespeople and the innocence of the investors. According to the SEC, "During the 1920s, approximately 20 million large and small shareholders took advantage of post-war prosperity and set out to make their fortunes in the stock market. It is estimated that

134. More of everything (*Steel Sparks*, December 31, 1920)

of the $50 billion in new securities offered during this period, half became worthless" (US Securities and Exchange Commission 2011).

Stock offerings were common during that time. Just outside of Buffalo in the village of East Aurora, the peaceful artisans of the Roycroft community were offering preferred stock in a way that should sound familiar to Steel's investors.

There were other problems with L. R.'s venture into the world of finance. First, and probably most significant, was his intentional targeting of small, unsophisticated investors. These people made a good customer

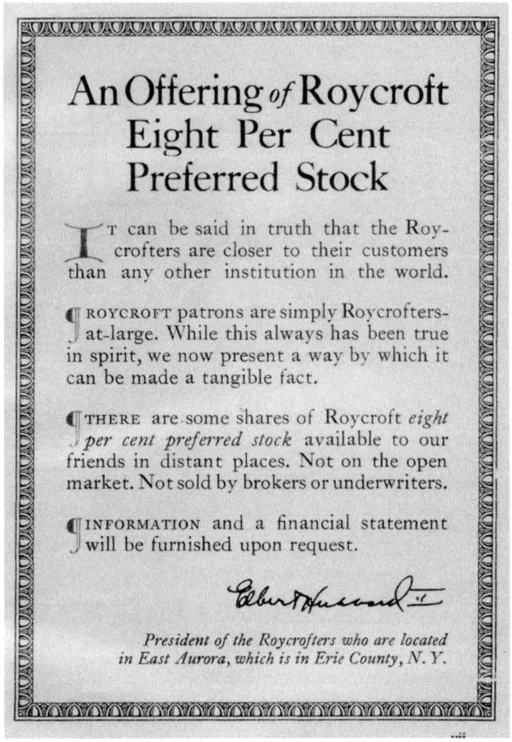

135. Stock offering (*Roycroft Magazine,* April 1921) (author's collection)

base for his stores, but they were not prepared to adequately evaluate the investment potential of his stock offering.

Today, stock in L. R.'s various companies would be called a private offering, a situation where stock is offered to only a select group of high–net worth investors. It is not registered with the SEC and does not trade on any exchange. Investors who participate should be sophisticated enough to understand the situation and the risks, but L. R.'s investors were not.

His investors thought they owned and controlled the company, but, actually, a controlling interest in every company was held by L. R. and he appointed the board of directors. It was accomplished, at least in part, by confusing the investors over the difference between preferred and common stock. Preferred stock sounds better, but actually it carried no voting rights. Only the common stock provided shareholders with a vote. In addition, investors could get common stock only if they bought the preferred. One share of common stock was given as a bonus when two shares of preferred were purchased.

Although the practice of issuing nonvoting stock may sound deceptive, it has actually become quite popular in Silicon Valley. Companies like Facebook, Google, and Groupon have done it because the original founders wanted to retain control while getting financing from the public. Their motivation was the same as L. R.'s.

The stock was not listed on any exchange, and L. R. tried to keep it from trading on any secondary markets. He wanted to be the only source for his stock so that he could control pricing. He occasionally wrote in the newsletter that brokers were trying to get people to sell their stock at low prices, a sign that its true value was much higher. The large stock holdings of the officers were mentioned as evidence of the commitment of management to the company.

There was no way for investors to sell their stock, but this important fact seemed too subtle for the sixty thousand investors. Also, there was no effective limit on the amount of stock that was issued. When it was all sold, they would either print more or start another company with a new stock offering. A potentially infinite supply of stock was being sold into a very illiquid market.

Finally, the commission-driven sales force worked with the patriotic zeal of the Liberty Bond campaign, their original template. With the moral certainty that they were providing a "service" to their customers by introducing them to this excellent investment, they were probably able to have their way with the prospects who had been recruited through L. R.'s infomercial.

A tongue-in-cheek article about Will Hahn's young son's stock scheme also sheds light on L. R.'s world. Young Horace Hahn has dug a hole in his backyard and now wants to sell stock in the enterprise. The Steelites probably loved the joke, but, like a lot of humor, it probably worked because it hinted at something that could not be said openly. The stores were better than a hole in the ground, but the Steelites may not have been sure how much better.

An excerpt from *Steel Sparks* provides some insight into L. R.'s fundamental problem: he thought he could print money. Of course, he would have been right if his company had been successful and profitable. Wealth really is created by economic activity. The economy is not a zero-sum game in which a fixed amount of money is traded back and forth between participants. Entrepreneurs like L. R. actually create new wealth; they do not just rearrange the chips around the poker table. L. R. could have made two and two equal five if his businesses had been profitable.

L. R. could have been more successful if he had taken the company public and let Wall Street handle the stock sales. The continuous feedback from the value of the stock trading in the open market might have motivated some discipline in his operations. This model worked well for Woolworth's, which went public in 1912 and raised thirty million dollars in capital to help expand its operations (Lebhar 1963, 12). Woolworth's became one of the thirty stocks in the Dow Jones Industrial Average and stayed in business until 1997. After closing the remaining five-and-dime stores, the company reorganized to focus on the athletic shoe market. This successor

HE NOW HAS HIS OWN SERVICE CORPORATION

Horace Hahn.

Although only five years old, Horace Hahn, son of Western District Manager William L. Hahn, has formed a company and service corporation at his home in Denver. In the rear yard of his home there is a "mine." It isn't very deep as yet, but "pay dirt" has been struck in sufficient quantities to warrant placing of the company's stock on the market. Shares are being sold by the "Horace Hahn Service Corporation" as fiscal agent for "The Horace Hahn Mining Company," there being 50,000 shares of preferred stock, par value Two Pins, with 5,000 shares of common stock, no par value. William L. Hahn is registrar and Raymond V. Hahn transfer agent. It is said there has been quite a flurry in the above stock recently and that is why W. H. Hahn rushed home from Buffalo to give the matter attention.

136. Will Hahn's son has his own stock scheme (*Steel Sparks,* April 23, 1921)

A THOUSAND DOLLAR BILL.

A piece of paper stamped by the Government becomes a thousand dollar bill. A piece of paper stamped by Steel Services becomes a thousand dollar certificate of shares—in time worth more than a thousand dollars by virtue of dividends and increased value of Steel Securities. There's value for you!!

137. Printing money (*Steel Sparks,* June 5, 1920)

company, Foot Locker, Inc., still trades on the New York Stock Exchange. This option would not, however, have been easy for L. R. in 1919 when he began the company. When Woolworth's went public, the company already had more than six hundred retail stores and was doing more than sixty million dollars in annual sales. Wall Street, especially in the 1920s, liked companies with a proven track record, not just ideas.

Wall Street also preferred industrial companies with obvious manufacturing capability. A good example is another company in Buffalo, Curtis Aeroplane and Motor Company, which went public in 1916. Founded by aviation pioneer Glenn Curtis, the company went on to build ten thousand airplanes for World War I. They are still in business, now making components rather than entire airplanes, and they are still on the New York Stock Exchange as Curtis-Wright Corporation.

Also, L. R. had a personal dislike for Wall Street. His former employer had denied him a promotion by bringing in a Wall Street banker with no retail experience to be president of the company. He did not want to rely on Wall Street when he thought he could do a better job raising his own money.

If the stock-selling enterprise had not been so easy, so lucrative, and so tempting, he actually might have been more successful. With his energy and creative talent focused only on the business, and without an addictive stream of easy money, he might have been more like Wal-Mart and less like Enron.

11

The Legacy of Failure

Life Goes on . . . or Not

FAILURE HAS CONSEQUENCES. Lives change. Businesses vanish. Buildings are reused.

The Business

At its zenith, Steel's had seventy-five retail locations in sixty-one cities, perhaps five thousand employees, and sixty thousand investors. There were also more than one hundred offices that supported the "service" organization in its mission to sell stock.

The sales offices closed immediately, and the salespeople drifted away. They had been encouraged by the company to put their savings into the stock they sold, so many of them had heavy losses. Some went back into teaching or factory work. Others went back home to live with their parents. Some stayed in the retail sector, but few seemed to have the inclination to remain in sales.

The bankruptcy petition was filed on April 30, 1923. Trustees were appointed, an audit was begun, and by May they started selling the real estate, first in Chicago and then in Kansas City and Pittsburgh. On December 3, 1923, the trustees accepted an offer for the Denver store. Architect Merrill Hoyt, who designed the Denver building, sued for unpaid fees. On April 24, 1924, the Syracuse store was sold.

The bankruptcy was messy, in part because of the size of the organization, the casual accounting standards, and the many angry shareholders. Two competing groups of investors argued with state officials, the receivers, and each other.

The list of creditors provides an interesting cross-section of small and large businesses that were providing products for the retail market in the early 1920s. The following is a selection with the amount owed to each:

- Alert Specialty Company, Buffalo, New York, $2.40
- American Crayon Company, Sandusky, Ohio, $61.96
- Art Crayon Company, New York City, $1.07
- Automatic Pencil Sharpener Company, Chicago, Illinois, $2.93
- Colgate & Company, New York City, $2,938.40
- Cracker Jack Company, Chicago, Illinois, $42.70
- Dixie Chemical Products, Birmingham, Alabama, $7.50
- Goshen Novelty & Lamp, Goshen, Indiana, $18.43
- Imperial Underwear Company, Scranton, Pennsylvania, $764.84
- Jiffy Jumper Manufacturing Company, Chicago, Illinois, $18.49
- Modern Neckwear Company, New York City, $20.38
- Oswego Corset Company, Oswego, New York, $547.73
- Pathe Phonograph and Radio Corporation, Brooklyn, New York, $1,052.48
- Perfection Biscuit Company, Fort Wayne, Indiana, $80.90
- Pyramid Playing Card Company, New York City, $350.04
- Roycrofters, East Aurora, New York, $170.25
- Shinola Company, Rochester, New York, $18.42
- Universal Powder Puff Company, Newark, New Jersey, $345.19
- Venus Petticoat Company, New York City, $17.25

Enough assets were sold to recover some money for the creditors. If they were due $15 or less, they got 80 percent of their money. Creditors who were owed more than $15 were paid 20 percent.

A shareholders' protective trust was established in an attempt to preserve some of the money from the investors. Investors were issued one share of stock in the protective trust for every share they had in the bankrupt company. The stock certificates were attractive, but they just provided false hope and, probably, more confusion.

On May 7, 1924, a petition was filed to discharge the bankruptcy and have the operation continue as Steel's Consolidated. About twenty stores were left, and Walter M. Wilkins was the president. On December 27, 1924, a board was appointed to determine whether there was any residual equity or unpaid dividends for the holders of the old stock (*New York Times* 1924). No payments were ever made, and there was no ready

No. 26616 2 Shares

L. R. STEEL
STOCKHOLDERS' PROTECTIVE TRUST

7% PREFERRED $10.00 PER SHARE

THIS IS TO CERTIFY that

is the owner of Two *fully paid and non-assessable shares in the L. R. STEEL STOCKHOLDERS' PROTECTIVE TRUST established under the provisions of a declaration of Trust dated April 14, 1923, filed in the office of the County Clerk of Erie County, New York, and a true copy of which is filed with the Peoples Bank of Buffalo as depositary. By acceptance of this certificate, the certificate holder herein named agrees that he participates in the trust upon the terms set forth in said declaration of trust.*

The interest of the certificate holder is transferable upon the books of the trustees in person or by attorney upon the surrender of this certificate.

Witness our hands this day October 20, 1924

Countersigned by

Transfer Clerk

Trustees L. R. Steel Stockholders' Protective Trust

138. Certificate from the shareholders' protective trust (author's collection)

market for the stock. Also, because most of the stock had been sold on a subscription basis, many investors forfeited their down payments rather than complete their purchases.

The stores continued in operation for a few years, but the magic was gone. There was no more income from stock sales, and the shoppers who had eagerly patronized the stores that they owned stock in were now understandably absent.

A second bankruptcy was filed in March 1930 (*Buffalo Courier Express* 1930). There was no possibility of recovering from this one with the onset of the Great Depression. There were twenty-three stores left, including one on Hertel Avenue in Buffalo. Walter M. Wilkins was still the president.

Some of L. R.'s ideas lived on. On the day after L. R. died, Henry Ford announced the purchase of 125,000 acres of coal land in eastern Kentucky from the F. S. Peabody syndicate. The $4 million investment was intended to provide a secure source of power for a growing business empire (*New York Times* 1923a).

Properties

The Denver Store

The Denver store lives on today. Of course, it is no longer called Steel's Corner, but it has been lovingly restored and has been given a new life as a commercial building strategically located at Sixteenth and Welton in downtown Denver.

For years, the building was known as the Fontius Building after a shoe manufacturing company that previously occupied it. The building deteriorated as it sat vacant for almost twenty years. It would have been torn down, but it had been designated as a historic building.

The building is now owned by Denver developer Evan Makovsky, who put together a public-private partnership to fund the $16.5 million restoration. The exterior work was finished just in time for the Democratic National Convention in August 2008. L. R. would have loved all the flags even though he was a staunch Republican.

139. Steel's Corner in 2008 (photo courtesy of Ken Schroeppel)

The current name is the Sage Building, after Sage Hospitality Resources, a Denver-based hotel developer that has leased the three upper floors as its corporate headquarters. The street level is occupied by several retail operations, including a coffee shop and a bank. The street has been turned into a pedestrian-only street as part of a project to redevelop a formerly blighted downtown area. Denver mayor John Hickenlooper said, "The City's economic development tools have spurred restoration of this incredible building, which, in turn, further activates our downtown, poising Denver for additional jobs" (Denver Office of Economic Development 2008). As L. R. clearly understood, it is always useful to keep the local politicians involved.

The Lafayette Hotel

The Lafayette Hotel was just down the street from Steel's headquarters and the Steel Cafeteria in Buffalo. It was the scene of many banquets, meetings, and surprise parties. It is still in operation under the same name and has been restored to its former glory. It is even listed on the National Register of Historic Places.

140. The Lafayette Hotel today (author's photo)

The Cafeteria in Buffalo

At least part of the building that housed the Steel Cafeteria in Buffalo is still standing. The location of the fire hydrant is the best clue, assuming it has not moved in ninety years. L. R. had been there on New Year's Eve to hand out cigars to the gentlemen and flowers to the ladies.

The Sugar Plantation

The five-hundred-acre plantation, including a sugar mill and various housing structures for the staff, was purchased for more than four hundred thousand dollars to provide a secure source of sugar for the Mary Lincoln Candy stores. When the company went into bankruptcy, this large asset had an outstanding mortgage balance of seventy-five thousand dollars. It initially looked like an asset that could be sold at a profit, but a heavy rain in southern Florida left most of the property under water. The receivers determined that the property could no longer be sold for enough to cover the mortgage, so they elected to keep paying the mortgage until a drainage canal could be finished.

141. The Steel's Cafeteria building in 2009 (photo by Dave Dyer)

The property suffered through a major hurricane in 1926 and eventually became inactive, but it is back in production today as part of the US Sugar Corporation.

Marguerite Manor

The acreage around Marguerite Manor had been turned into a chicken farm that was owned by Steel's Farms Produce Division, but the beautiful home on Getzville Road just north of Buffalo remained as part of L. R.'s estate. It was purchased by a local businessman named Hans Geyer.

Geyer, who had emigrated from Australia in 1896, turned the home into a restaurant with a dance hall and hotel out behind. Called the Chateau, it was a popular nightspot that featured live jazz entertainment provided by a "Negro Orchestra" that was housed in the top floor of the hotel.

After about a year of success, a fire destroyed the business in 1926 (*Buffalo Courier Express* 1926a). The dance hall and hotel were destroyed, and Marguerite Manor was damaged. Arson was suspected, and a reward was offered for information. Geyer had invested his life savings in developing the business and had no insurance.

Marguerite Manor seems to have been restored after the fire because there was a second fire in 1938 (*Buffalo Courier Express* 1938). This fire totally destroyed the structure. The unoccupied home had recently been rented to the St. Rita Society to be used as a convalescent home for children. The fire, which was thought to have been caused by a short circuit, lasted for more than an hour, and flames could be seen from several miles away. In a final indignity, the local newspaper got L. R.'s name wrong, referring to him as "L. R. Steele." It was the last reference to him in any publication.

I tried to find the spot where Marguerite Manor was located, but that part of Getzville Road no longer exists. The area has been rearranged by the development of the north campus of the State University of New York at Buffalo and an interchange for the Lockport Expressway.

The Movie

There were fifty copies of the movie in circulation, with ten reels in each. They were in towns all over North America and were probably not returned in an orderly fashion when the company collapsed. I hoped to find a copy, but I was not that lucky. The last known showing was to investigators in the Erie County Courthouse who were looking for evidence of fraud. It may still be in some evidence storage area, but I could not locate it. By now, the film would have deteriorated. Some of the old films were melted down for their silver content, so that may have happened. Still, perhaps in an attic or closet of a descendant of someone who ran an old movie house . . .

People

Marguerite Steel

When L. R.'s estate was finally settled (*Buffalo Courier Express* 1926b), there was no money left for his wife, despite the generous bequest in his will. The estate was valued at $17,399, but the legal expenses to administer the estate and untangle his affairs came to $9,319. L. R. died before paying his federal income tax for 1922, and that bill was $76,722. Uncle Sam lost about $60,000 in unpaid taxes, and Marguerite got nothing.

Marguerite had a difficult time without L. R. At age forty, she is listed in the 1930 census. She went from living in an estate named after her to living in a rooming house in Lockport, New York, with seven other roomers. The rooming house included a lady who was a cashier at restaurant and a man who was a railroad worker. Marguerite listed her occupation as "practical nurse" in a private home. She was probably emptying bed pans for some people who were even worse off than she was. Her son, Philip, was not listed as living there, but he would have been twenty-one by then.

She never remarried and kept out of the news. In 1957, at age sixty-seven, she joined L. R. in Forest Lawn (*Buffalo Evening News* 1957). Her cremated remains were scattered on her husband's grave.

Philip Steel

Philip, the adopted son of L. R. and Marguerite, did not seem to pick up any of L. R.'s ambition. When he signed up for Social Security in 1937, he was unemployed at age twenty-six and living in Buffalo. It was easy to be unemployed during the Depression, but I expect L. R. would have started a business or found some other way to make money.

He died in his Studio City, California, apartment in January 1984 at age seventy-three. He had gone into the movie business, sort of. He was an electrician for Universal Studios.

Will Hahn and His Son, Horace

L. R.'s protégé, Will Hahn, also moved to California. In the 1930 census, he was living in Los Angeles and working as the general manager of a washing machine company. He had a new wife who was nine years younger than he was, and his adopted son, Horace, was fourteen.

Unlike Philip, Horace had an ambitious streak. Perhaps that enterprising attitude was illustrated by his early playful attempt to sell shares in a hole in his backyard when he lived in Denver. He went to the University of California at Los Angeles, where he was a debating champion, and then to Stanford Law School. He was a decorated intelligence officer in World War II, and after the war, he helped prosecute the Nazi war criminals at the Nuremberg War Trials. He practiced law in California for fifty years and helped found two prominent law firms. He died in 2003 at the age of eighty-seven (*Idyllwild Town Crier* 2003).

Walter M. Wilkins

Walter M. Wilkins fared well after the collapse of the company. He came away from the bankruptcy as the president of the new organization, Steel's Consolidated. Also, his legal problems went away when the indictment was thrown out by the courts, so he was free to continue his career. When Steel's Consolidated went out of business in 1930, he became an Erie County assistant district attorney, hired by the same person who had indicted him in 1923. However, his good fortune ended in 1936 with an untimely death at age fifty as the result of complications from an operation.

His obituary in the Buffalo newspaper (*Buffalo Courier Express* 1936) detailed a successful career, including being managing editor of the *Daily Princetonian* and president of the student council while earning a degree from Princeton. To complete his blue-ribbon credentials, he received his law degree from Harvard in 1913. After law school, he returned to Buffalo and joined the law firm of Kenefick, Cooke, Mitchell, and Bass. Then the obituary makes an odd error. After seven years with the law firm, it claims he became an assistant district attorney in 1922 and continued there until his death. Even though the same newspaper had reported on his career with Steel's between 1922 and 1930, someone clearly wanted to forget that bit of history.

The Employees

Working at Steel's was probably the personal high point of many people's lives. It was fun, they were part of an exciting adventure, and they made a lot of money. Everyone loved the boss. There were big parties, fresh flowers every day, a lot of camaraderie, and the occasional singalong. New opportunities came with every new stock offering and every new office that needed a manager. Women had as much opportunity as men, as long as they brought in contracts.

HITTING THE HIGH MARKS

Miss Eva Fritsch, one of the three 50-share Service Button winners who helped to establish a new high production record for Division F of the Greater New York office for the week ended April 22, putting that division again in the lead in the United States. Sincere congratulations to Miss Fritsch on the fine work she is doing.

142. Eva Fritsch (*Steel Sparks,* April 29, 1922)

Eva Fritsch's experience may have been typical. Her obvious beauty probably helped her set the new production record for her division. They put her in the company newsletter, and she would certainly have been asked to give a speech at the next dinner party. She earned an excellent income, as much as a man who had sold as many shares as she did. For a while, at least, she probably made as much money as a physician or an attorney. Her coworkers admired and respected her. She must have been very happy.

I found her in the 1930 census, just at the start of the Great Depression. She was single and living alone in a rooming house in Pittsburgh while working as a clerk at an insurance company. At thirty-four, she was probably beyond a marriageable age for those times. The census reveals that she emigrated from Germany in 1922. Steel's must have been her first job in America. I hope she enjoyed it while it lasted.

My Great-Uncle, Clayton Pickard

Finally, I return to my original motivation. Why did my great-uncle, Clayton Pickard, vanish in 1923?

Shame and embarrassment are powerful emotions. No one wants to think that they were part of a venture that cost thousands of people their life savings. That point is probably why Walter M. Wilkins's eight years with Steel's did not appear in his obituary. I am sure it also played a role in Clayton's disappearance.

Because Buffalo was still a boomtown, he decided to stay there. He had traveled so much with Steel's that he probably did not know many people there. It would not be hard to change his identity even if he stayed in Buffalo. He changed his last name from Pickard to Picard and changed his ethnicity to French Canadian. He lived quietly with his own mystery. He certainly had no idea that his sister's grandson would devote so much time to finding him.

Failure has consequences. People make decisions, not always good ones.

Postscript

> The line between success and failure is so finely drawn that often all that is required is one step forward to land on the winning side.
>
> —L. R. Steel, December 24, 1920

WE ALWAYS HEAR ABOUT THE WINNERS; this book is about the losers.

We have all heard the rags-to-riches stories told by those who succeed against the odds. We have heard the inspirational messages about how anyone can do it with hard work, frugality, honesty, perseverance, and a good heart. Everybody knows that story.

We never hear from the losers, especially the losers who had all the talent and dedication to win, who should have won, but did not. Those people can be more interesting than the ones who won.

L. R. Steel was one of those losers. His company could have been Wal-Mart, but it ended up more like Enron. He died penniless at only forty-four with all of his net worth in his own company's worthless stock.

Thousands of Steel's employees lost their jobs.

All sixty thousand investors lost everything that they invested.

Everybody lost everything.

And my great-uncle, Clayton, lost his family.

If L. R. had been just a huckster or scam artist, this story would have little interest. But he was a creative genius who foresaw the value of corporate charity, hiring and promoting women, vertical integration taken to an extreme, and creative financing that actually resulted in building a new four-story building with funds contributed by his own employees. And, of course, he invented the infomercial. He should have been a success.

References

Index

References

Allen, Frederick Lewis. 1931. *Only Yesterday: An Informal History of the 1920's.* New York: HarperCollins.

Buffalo Courier Express. 1923. "Leonard R. Steel Buried in Forest Lawn Cemetery." Mar. 25.

———. 1926a. "Hans Geyer's Big Chateau Is in Ashes; Fire Levels Home of Late L. R. Steel on Getzville Rd." Dec. 13.

———. 1926b. "L. R. Steel's Assets Will Go for Taxes; U.S. Whistles for $60,000 Due." Oct. 14.

———. 1930. "Court Names Receivers for Steel's Stores, Inc." Mar. 26.

———. 1936. "Death Takes W. M. Wilkins." Dec. 24.

———. 1938. "Old Mansion of L. R. Steele Fire-Swept, Loss Is $20,000." June 27.

Buffalo Evening News. 1957. Obituary of Marguerite Steel. Dec. 10.

Buffalo Express. 1923. "L. R. Steel Indicted Here April, 1917, It Appears." Mar. 23.

Buffalo Times. 1923. "Lay Leonard R. Steel at Rest; 350 Mourners Crowd Getzville Home." Mar. 25.

Collins, Jim. 2009. *How the Mighty Fall and Why Some Companies Never Give In.* New York: HarperCollins.

Denver Office of Economic Development. 2008. "Sage Hospitality to Relocate to Historic Steel Building." June 11. http://www.denvergov.org/oed/DenverOfficeofEconomicDevelopment/Newsroom/tabid/435773/newsid488087/3741/Sage-Hospitality-to-Relocate-to-Historic-Steel-Building/Default.aspx.

Erie County Supreme Court. *The People of the State of New York v. Walter M. Wilkins.* Nov. 5, 1926.

Everson, William K. 1998. *American Silent Film.* New York: Da Capo Press.

Gifford, R. E. 1922. *Pennsylvania Hills to the Chain of Steel Industries: A Story of Industry.* New York: L. R. Steel Service.

House, A., et al. 1990. "Life Events and Difficulties Preceding Stroke." *Journal of Neurology, Neurosurgery, and Psychiatry* 53: 1024–28.

Idyllwild Town Crier. 2003. Obituary of Horace Hahn. Dec. 5.

Infoplease. 2011. "Population of the 20 Largest U.S. Cities, 1900–2005." Family Education Network. http://www.infoplease.com/ipa/A0922422.html.

Inter IKEA Systems B.V. 2011. "The IKEA Store." http://franchisor.ikea.com/showContent.asp?swfId=store1.

Lebhar, Godfrey M. 1963. *Chain Stores in America, 1859–1962*. New York: Chain Store Publishing.

Maney, Kevin. 2003. *The Maverick and His Machine: Thomas Watson Sr. and the Making of IBM*. Hoboken, NJ: John Wiley and Sons.

New York Times. 1923a. "Ford to Buy More Coal." Mar. 23. http://select.nytimes.com/gst/abstract.html?res=F70912FB385516738DDDAA0A94DB405B838EF1D3&scp=3&sq=peabody&st=p.

———. 1923b. "L. R. Steel Retires from All Concerns." Jan. 28. http://select.nytimes.com/gst/abstract.html?res=FB0A16FF3D5416738DDDA10A94D9405B838EF1D3&scp=1&sq=steel&st=p.

———. 1923c. "Sherman Ends Stock Sales." Mar. 2. http://select.nytimes.com/gst/abstract.html?res=F40717FA3D5416738DDDAB0894DB405B838EF1D3&scp=2&sq=steel&st=p.

———. 1923d. "Stops Sale of Stock." Feb. 22. http://select.nytimes.com/gst/abstract.html?res=FB0F16F7395516738DDDAB0A94DA405B838EF1D3&scp=3&sq=steel&st=p.

———. 1924. "L. R. Steel Plans Drawn; Board May Save Something for the Holders of the Old Stock." Dec. 28. http://select.nytimes.com/gst/abstract.html?res=F70C13FF3C551B7A93CAAB1789D95F408285F9&scp=6&sq=steel&st=p.

Plunkett-Powell, Karen. 1999. *Remembering Woolworth's*. New York: St. Martin's Press.

Toledo Blade. 1923. "L. R Steel Stricken on Train in Toledo." Mar. 22.

United States Investor. 1921. "L. R. Steel Figures." May 7. http://books.google.com/books?id=q7RLAQAAIAAJ&pg=RA1-PA30&lpg=RA1PA30&dq=%22L.R.+Steel+Company%22&source=bl&ots=oOK2wHmtJR&sig=Q37959T4OM4swq154kwWM1G8js&hl=en&sa=X&ei=7PgbT6qrD6X40gHDgJ3hCw&sqi=2&ved=0CDwQ6AEwAw#v=onepage&q=%22L.R.%20Steel%20Company%22&f=false.

US Census Bureau. 1998. "Population of the 100 Largest Urban Places: 1920." Table 15. http://www.census.gov/population/www/documentation/twps0027/tab15.txt.

———. 2000. "New York, Place and County Subdivision, GCT-PH1. Population, Housing Units, Area, and Density: 2000." Data Set: Census 2000, Summary File 1. http://factfinder.census.gov/servlet/GCTTable?_bm=y&-geo_id=04000US36&-_box_head_nbr=GCT-PH1&-ds_name=DEC_2000_SF1_U&-format=ST-7.

US Department of Labor, Bureau of Labor Statistics. 2011. "CPI Inflation Calculator." http://data.bls.gov/cgi-bin/cpicalc.pl.

US Securities and Exchange Commission. 2011. "Creation of the SEC." http://www.sec.gov/about/whatwedo.shtml.

Vance, Sandra S., and Roy V. Scott. 1994. *Wal-Mart: A History of Sam Walton's Retail Phenomenon.* New York: Twayne.

Zuckoff, Mitchell. 2005. *Ponzi's Scheme.* New York: Random House.

Background Reading

British Film Institute. Archives. http://www.bfi.org.uk/ (accessed Feb. 2, 2012).

Dillaway, Diana. 2006. *Power Failure: Politics, Patronage, and the Economic Future of Buffalo, New York.* Amherst, NY: Prometheus Books.

Dunn, Donald. 1975. *Ponzi: The Incredible True Story of the King of Financial Cons.* New York: Random House.

George Eastman House International Museum of Photography and Film. Archives. http://www.eastmanhouse.org/ (accessed Feb. 2, 2012).

Goldberg, Ronald Allen. 2003. *America in the Twenties.* Syracuse: Syracuse Univ. Press.

Goldman, Mark. 2007. *City on the Edge: Buffalo, New York.* Amherst, NY: Prometheus Books.

Hayward, Walter Sumner, Percival White, John Sherwood Fleek, and Harry McIntyre. 1922. *Chain Stores: Their Management and Operation.* New York: McGraw-Hill.

Kogan, Herman, and Rick Kogan. 1989. *Pharmacist to the Nation: A History of Walgreen Co.* Deerfield, IL: Walgreen.

Kresge, Stanley S. 1979. *The S. S. Kresge Story.* Racine, WI: Western Publishing.

Lewis, Sinclair. 1922. *Babbitt.* New York: Penguin.

Moody's Manual of Railroads and Corporation Securities. 1922. Industrial Section, vol. 2, twenty-third annual issue. New York: Poor's Publishing.

Mowry, George E., ed. 1963. *The Twenties: Fords, Flappers, and Fanatics.* Englewood Cliffs, NJ: Prentice-Hall.

Rizzo, Michael F. 2007. *Nine Nine Eight: The Glory Days of Buffalo Shopping.* Morrisville, NC: Lulu Enterprises.

Roycroft Magazine (East Aurora, NY), Sept. 1917–Apr. 1922.

Russell, Francis. 1964. *The Great Interlude: Neglected Events and Persons from the First World War to the Depression.* New York: McGraw-Hill.

———. 1968. *The Shadow of Blooming Grove: Warren G. Harding in His Times.* New York: McGraw-Hill.

Index